Stamps
for
Investment

Stamps for Investment

KENNETH R. LAKE

𝕾𝕯 STEIN AND DAY/*Publishers*/New York

CONTENTS

1806200

Stamps for Investment

INTRODUCTION

THIS BOOK was completed as the Great Air Race organized by the London *Daily Mail* ended. For eight days men and women had sped from the Empire State Building to London's Post Office Tower in many ingenious ways, and speed records were broken again and again.

Neither country issued special stamps for this marathon, but several of the aircraft taking part carried small quantities of mail. Such "flown covers," as they are called, received special handstamps and cachets indicating their status, in addition to ordinary stamps of the United States or Great Britain, and some bear pilots' signatures and other interesting markings.

The demand for these covers far outran the supply, and when they were offered for sale at auction—by dealers or collectors canny or lucky enough to obtain them—prices in excess of $30 were usual. And all this for simple envelopes, dressed up with printed cachets and bearing regular stamps with a few hand-stamped marks!

What is the appeal of such items to the collector and the investor? Why should a cover costing perhaps 30 cents to prepare soar to a hundred times its value within days, while attractive stamps sold by the U. S. Post Office twenty years ago are still available in quantity at less than face value—despite the fall in the value of money over that period?

Philately poses many questions like this to the newcomer, and even the expert never stops learning. A $2.60 stamp issued in 1930 is now catalogued at $300, but a $5 stamp issued seven years earlier is listed at only $31.50. And the 1930 stamp, if you are lucky enough to have it in a block of four stamps from the corner of the sheet, with a number in the margin, catalogues at not just four times the price of a single stamp but at the astonishing price of $2,250!

But if all this sounds alluring, stop and consider that first-day covers specially prepared by reputable dealers, costing far more than the stamps they bear and neatly postmarked at no inconsiderable expense to the dealer at the one city chosen for that honor, are available in later years so cheaply that many dealers soak off the stamps and sell them by the thousands for inclusion in children's packets, destroying the covers as worthless. Yet the novice still goes on buying them in the belief that he is going to make enough money to retire on or to put his son through college. It is this ignorance which the present book seeks to dispel, by explaining how the stamp market works.

London and New York are the twin centers of the world's stamp market. The annual turnover is immeasurable; one auction house, with branches in both cities, sold more than $3.5 million in the 1967–68 season alone. London, with the biggest market, the biggest auctioneers and retail merchants, and the biggest wholesaler in Europe, has a more diversified trade than anywhere else. Over a third of the stamps sold in London go overseas, and many are imported merely to resell on the best market. New York's business is directed more to the domestic market, but the amounts of money which change hands there affect the international market.

Stamps, as an investment and as a hobby, are becoming more popular every year, and offer an unrivaled field for enjoyment and profit—provided one understands what one is doing.

Nobody would expect to make money from a trade, profession, or hobby without some degree of study. No thinking man would base an investment portfolio simply on hunch, on personal prejudice, or on the recommendation of the firms issuing the shares. Yet many stamp collectors do all these things, and still naïvely expect to make their collections pay handsome dividends. Even the gambler who picks horses with a pin stands a better chance than this—the field is smaller, and in every race *one* horse must win.

I am an enthusiastic collector and a philatelic writer with an interest in all fields of collecting and investment. As P.R.O. and Advertising Manager of Stanley Gibbons Ltd., and formerly as Advertisement Manager of the independent weekly magazine *Stamp Collecting,* I came into contact daily with both dealers and collectors. My intention in writing this book is to promote healthy investment on both sides of the Atlantic, to aid the collector in both countries in bettering his collection, and to help the potential investor make the best use of his money.

Sensible investment benefits the stamp trade and the collector. Irresponsible investment, based on irrational prejudices, misinformation, or ignorance, can have severe repercussions on the image of both trade and hobby, and its effect on the pocketbook of the unwary investor can be catastrophic.

In this book you will find few references to countries whose stamps are already booming, and few quotations of current market or catalogue prices. Up-to-date information of this type can be gained by reading philatelic magazines and by personal experience. My aim is to show *how* things happen, *why* the market functions as it does, and to offer some tips on what is likely to happen in years to come.

ENJOY YOUR

SPENDING

STAMP COLLECTING is an enjoyable hobby. Because it is a hobby, one of the most potent influences on the stamp market is popularity, and the countries whose stamps today top the market are those which are currently enjoying a vogue among collectors and investors.

I shall examine some of the reasons for popularity in a moment; first I want to stress that, because of the ebb and flow of a country's philatelic popularity, *no* stamps can be guaranteed to rise in value year by year forever, and conversely *no* stamp need be forever written off as a complete loss. There are "blue chips," and there are also millions of stamps for which the only rise in cost over twenty years is likely to be that caused by inflation. But between these two there are many, many issues which, with knowledge as the pathway, can be turned to profit.

Prophecy is a dangerous profession. Certain short-term investments can be picked out at any time, and some broad trends of development can be foreseen with fair assurance. But the careful investor keeps his eye on the market week by week and watches for fresh indications of market movements before the general collecting public flocks to the flag. The aim of this book is to show you how the market works, and why it moves as it does; armed with this knowledge you can become your own market tipster.

As a hobbyist you can learn to pick those countries whose stamps will give you the most pleasure with the best chance of realizing a profit. As an investor you will be better armed to judge what to buy and when to sell—and at the same time you will find much more enjoyment in stamps than you could in any other field of investment.

You cannot really mount stock certificates in an album and feel pleasure in looking at them. You can't spend your money on golf clubs or gliding, on theatrical make-up or racing-car maintenance, in the expectation of reaping a profit from your expenditure at a later date, unless you become a professional.

Many stamp hobbyists run sideline collections as an investment, or buy additional copies of stamps in their own specialized field which they feel are likely to provide a reliable profit. By doing this, they can feed their real collecting needs by occasionally selling off the investment property. Carried out intelligently and with insight, this system can enable a collector of modest means to build an ordinary collection into an award-winning one.

Many collectors make their purchases purely with an eye to future profit, and as they generally lack knowledge of the finer points of philately, they usually rely on the advice of a dealer or an investment consultant. In this way the investor may minimize his risk, but he loses a great deal of the pleasure that real collecting gives.

Overzealous study can be a pitfall for some collectors; their attention to philatelic minutiae blinds them to a stamp's poor investment potential. Yet such collectors at least have the consolation of the collection itself and the pleasure it has given them, whereas unsuccessful investment in most other fields leaves the sufferer with little but regret.

The investor who can dispose of upward of $20,000 a year on stamps stands in quite a different relationship to the market from the man who wants to put $5 a week into the hobby. Yet there is scope for both types; profit and enjoyment await the man at either end of the scale. The large-scale investor will, however, be buying quite a different class of material, for in stamps it is generally true to say that single expensive items, carefully chosen, appreciate more speedily and more safely than a multitude of smaller and cheaper items.

Regardless of the amount of money you are going to spend on stamps, you must know what you are buying. You must know what is meant by new issues, classics, market value and catalogue value (quite different things), blocked values, cancelled-to-order and cancelled-by-favor material (again two different things), limited issues, speculation, agency manipulation, restricted sale—all these affect the investment potential of a stamp. You must study postal history as well as market quotations, and consider the popularity, economic conditions, political developments, and philatelic policy of your chosen countries. Above all, you must know the principles of stamp dealing, which differ significantly from dealing in most other commodities.

If this all sounds rather dull and heavy, be assured that it isn't! I have said that stamp collecting is a hobby, and an enjoyable one: the more you know about these things the more you will appreciate your collection.

The best and most valuable collections in the world were all assembled for pleasure. King George V started the Royal Collection and found in it his greatest relaxation from the affairs of state. President Franklin D. Roosevelt was an ardent philatelist; he even appears on a stamp with his albums, the contents of which now grace many famous collections throughout the world. Yet the average collector can spend as little as $5 a week and gain not only immense satisfaction but also a worthwhile investment which he would have found impossible in any other field of endeavor.

Were stamp investment purely a hedge against inflation and a means of making profit, I would advise against it. But as an enjoyable hobby which can be made almost self-supporting, allied to sensible investment which should provide a worthwhile nest-egg, philately cannot be beaten. The recent world-wide growth in interest in stamp collecting both as hobby and as investment, together with the rising tide of affluence throughout the world, and particularly in countries hitherto classed as "have-nots," reinforces this statement.

But still the one great dictum stands: *Know what you are buying.*

BUYING

NEW ISSUES

THE COLLECTOR who bought in late 1960 a 2s.8d. (30 cents) stamp from Norfolk Island, issued to mark the introduction of local government to that far-off speck in the Pacific, was probably just keeping up with his new issues.

He probably bought one mint stamp, or one used copy, or one of each. A few collectors would have put away, as a matter of faith, a block of four copies. The number of collectors or investors who salted away full sheets of eighty stamps, at a cost in U.S. currency of $23.90 (plus dealer's commission) must have been very small indeed. After all, the face value of the stamp was considered unreasonably high, the country was not a popular one and had recently been much criticized in the philatelic press for its policy of producing too many new issues aimed purely at the collector, and there were a lot more "likely" items to attract the investor.

For some years the issue hung fire in the market; then suddenly the rise started, catching most collectors unaware. As I write this, a fair retail price for the stamp is $17 (mint) —well on the way to the cost of a full sheet of eighty stamps less than ten years ago! This is an extreme example, but the current market value of all Norfolk Island stamps issued in 1960 averages out at twenty times the face value, and the collector who acquired all ten new issues of Norfolk Island in 1960, at a cost of about $1.60, has now a holding retailing at around $30.

But one must also look at the other side of the coin. In 1964 Sierra Leone issued the world's first self-adhesive "freeform" stamps—a set of fourteen stamps, each the shape of the country and mounted on colored paper from which it could be peeled to affix directly to the envelope without licking. The face value of the set was $4.90, and at first sales were fairly brisk at around $6. Three years later odd values could be picked up at one-tenth face value, and when sets were offered through the trade on one memorable occasion for $1 each there were no takers—nobody wanted them!

We can now take the case a little further, by pointing out that changes in popularity could freeze the Norfolk Island "Local Government" stamp at its current price, and later bring it down again to perhaps a figure of $5 a copy. Then, some future craze may bring the despised "lickystickies" into fashion, and they might then rise well past their original face value and perhaps even realize up to $25 a set.

Both suggestions are unlikely—but neither is totally impossible. In later chapters we shall discuss how and why such things can happen. At present we are concerned with "new issues" hot from the presses of the security printers.

It is often said that one cannot lose by buying new issues. Fortunately, this is not true. If it were, the pressure of investment in new issues would long ago have killed the market.

It is certainly true to say that if one collects the stamps of any "living" country he will, in the long run, acquire all the stamps more cheaply by buying them from a reliable dealer against a standing-order new-issue service than by waiting until they become obsolete or until odd copies come his way. If this sounds a little facile in light of the Sierra Leone set I mentioned, I should point out that subsequent changes in that country's currency and philatelic policy brought forth a number of provisional issues of low face value but considerable scarcity. Purchase of these as new issues might have been made for about 75 cents—and they were retailing at well over $35 within months of issue.

So we see that this expenditure for new issues, regularly disbursed, can be regarded as an investment against possible fluctuations which cannot be foreseen at time of issue. It is not a sure-fire profit maker, but it is insurance against the unexpected. And, like any other insurance, it should be transacted through a reliable agent.

Many dealers run new-issue services. According to the terms of the agreement between the dealer and client, the stamps supplied may be mint or used, or on first-day covers; they may be single copies, blocks of four, or full sheets. The order may cover one country or many; it may include the supply of all *new* printings of regular stamps, which may differ only minutely from the last printing; it may include or exclude certain classes of stamps such as postage-dues or official stamps . . . the permutations are endless.

The operation of such a service involves the dealer in considerable outlay of capital with only a small profit (collectors as a breed are miserly in the commission they are prepared to pay a dealer and often slow to make payment for stamps received). Although most dealers demand a sizable deposit before any stamps are supplied, few can make a living solely from this service. They regard it as a loss leader to obtain new clients for other material on which the mark-up is higher, as a stimulant to investment in older material of the same countries of which they may have large stocks, and as a means of obtaining occasional scarce items direct from the issuing bodies at the face value—providing them with a windfall which would not otherwise come their way.

New issues of the United States can, of course, be bought at the post office or from the Philatelic Bureau in Washington. Those for Great Britain are supplied (to dealers only) by StanGib Limited, in New York, while new stamps of many countries in the British Commonwealth are supplied to dealers by the Crown Agents (at Sutton, in England) at their face value plus a standard handling charge. New issues of other countries may be supplied on similar terms from official governmental or private agencies in the United States or abroad; for some countries, application must be made direct to the postal administration of the country.

In all cases, business is on a strict prepayment basis. The dealer must maintain considerable credit balances with a number of postal administrations and agencies, as well as covering mailing fees, cables, and other incidental charges in arranging his orders.

Some countries issue "limited releases," available only against a large purchase of other items. Special issues often appear with little or no warning, necessitating the speedy remittance of large funds to ensure supplies.

Occasionally an issue may be made available in quantities too small to fill even the standing-order demands of the world's dealers. Advance warning of this possibility may cause the larger wholesalers to increase their normal orders, thus making supplies even scarcer. In such cases the smaller dealer may find that his order is arbitrarily cut and he must go cap in hand to the "big boys" to obtain, at far higher prices, stamps which he has already contracted to supply to his customers at normal new-issue rates. If the dealer is unable to carry the loss, he will of course put up his prices, but this may well cost him future orders when his customers learn that other dealers did in fact supply the stamps at the normal rates.

Then there is the question of condition. The knowledge-able collector will refuse stamps which are creased or which have damaged perforations. More discerning collectors will insist that all their stamps be perfectly centered—the perforations must be at equal distance from the stamp design on all four sides. A dealer cannot in most cases specify such perfect condition when ordering from a postal administration, whose only concern is to supply postage; consequently he may find that large stocks of stamps received against his standing order are unacceptable to many of his regular customers, and he is again driven to purchase on the open market at the prevailing price.

The supply of "fine-used" new issues to standing order often involves the dealer in further worries. A fine-used stamp is one with a light, clean, circular postmark which does not damage the stamp or obscure its design. To rely on commercial mail for such material, especially from small countries with little overseas mail, is useless, so depending on the country concerned, the dealer has two options: to avail himself of either a cancellation-to-order or a cancellation-by-favor service.

Many countries, particularly those in the Communist bloc, provide an official cancellation-to-order service. The postal authorities, or the trading agency, arrange to have full sheets of stamps postmarked, often by machine, before they ever reach a post office; these sheets are then made available to the trade at a cost far below the face value of the stamps. It goes without saying that such stamps are not suitable for investment: they are produced in vast quantities for the "packet trade," to be made up into lots for sale to junior collectors. Occasionally a country will resort to this practice to sell off stocks of older issues for which there is little demand at the full mint cost.

Other countries pursue different policies, and the collector should always find out for himself the real status of "used" stamps before accepting catalogue valuations as a true guide.

In the case of Australia, where "specimen sets" are officially made up, containing c-t-o copies of all definitive stamps up to 5 shillings face value and also high values with a neat "Specimen" overprint, the existence of vast quantities of commercially used copies of the low values makes the c-t-o copies equally cheap (but a dealer may charge a small premium for their finer condition).

For a time, stamps of Norfolk Island and other Australian External Territories were included in Specimen sets; here, however, supplies of commercially used material are so small that the c-t-o material carries the same high quotation as postally used material, both in the catalogue and from a dealer.

In the case of North Borneo, where remainders have been on offer in juniors' packets for over sixty years, Scott's catalogue has an introductory note warning collectors about c-t-o issues, but admitting that regardless of their provenance they have a market value.

Finally, in the case of Ghana, where remaining stocks of earlier issues were cancelled to order by the government in 1961, Scott's lists used valuations in italics for these re-mainders and states that genuine postally used copies are worth more.

The whole situation is therefore unclear and dangerous, and for this reason the investor is warned against c-t-o stamps.

"Cancelled-by-favor" stamps are quite a different thing. As we have seen, a dealer cannot expect to rely on com-mercial mail to provide him speedily with adequate mate-rial for his fine-used standing-order clients, especially where the smaller countries are concerned. What he does is to make use, either directly or through his wholesaler, of the services of a local agent. This man will buy large quantities of mint stamps and have them cancelled at the post office before sending them to the dealer. Naturally the agent charges for this service, and it is this additional charge which adds to the retail price of fine-used stamps of minor countries.

In having the stamps postmarked, the agent may have to affix them to self-addressed envelopes and subsequently soak off the stamps on receipt from the post office. He may be permitted to affix them to sheets of paper and have these handed directly back over the counter to him. He may even be able to have sheets postmarked exactly as they were sold to him, with full gum on the back.

To the purist, none of these constitutes proper postal use, since the cancellations are applied "by favor" purely for the purpose of supplying collectors. However, such stamps when sold are usually indistinguishable from postally used copies and it would be a rare collector who would refuse cleanly postmarked stamps in favor of hideously marked but more obviously commercial copies!

Nevertheless, one cannot deny that genuine commercial covers, correctly franked and postmarked and perhaps bearing other transit postmarks showing their passage across the world, will always command a considerable premium over single-used stamps in such cases. But this aspect will be discussed more fully later.

Most new-issue services operate on a fixed percentage basis. For mint stamps this may vary from 17 to 25 percent over the face value or the cost to the dealer. In some cases, limited issues are available to the dealer only if purchased together with large quantities of other stamps; the dealer's cost must therefore include a write-off against the cost of this unwanted material. For used stamps the new-issue cost will vary according to the country and, for large countries with a considerable quantity of commercial mail, dealers may well refuse to offer a new-issue service because it could not compete with the low-priced material which would come on the market as stocks built up. One can expect to pay from 33 to 100 percent over the face value for fine-used copies of stamps from out-of-the-way countries.

The major point to arise from all this is that it pays to place a regular standing order with a reliable dealer who has adequate capital to ensure his being able to supply *all* new issues, regardless of their cost or restricted release and regardless of any actual or artificial shortage of particular

issues, regularly and satisfactorily at a standard mark-up on
face or cost. The dealer who offers a cut-price service will
very often fall down on the very items which will cost most
to obtain after the event—the unannounced limited issues
and provisionals which are sought at the same time by every
dealer, investor, and collector, and which may already have
been subject to large-scale speculation or deliberate over-
ordering.

So it just does not pay, in the long run, to skimp on a
new-issue service. Having established that, the question
arises: Which new issues are likely to be the best investment?

Factors to be considered include popularity, possible future popularity, political changes and economic development
in the country of origin, the quantities issued, the post use
made of the stamps, speculation, and the general philatelic
policy of the country's postal administration or its agency.
All of these must be looked at closely.

TIPPING

NEW ISSUES

"I particularly like the prospects of the Samoan 20/10s. Kingsford Smith issue of 1968. A stamp which should be obtained at once—and try to get it used."

THE QUOTATION is from the weekly market feature in *Stamp Collecting* by "W. E. Fyndem." There have been several "Fyndems" over the years, each a highly experienced writer with a knowledge of the whole field of philatelic investment.

Sometimes the market tipster's comment is that a stamp will improve within a matter of weeks; sometimes it is a long-term tip for slow appreciation over a number of years. Occasionally it is a hunch, naming a stamp which may not move at all for a long, long time but is worth putting away for the future.

The tipster's column is one of the most popular in any philatelic journal, and the one which most readers turn to first—even before they scan the news pages. But, of course, no tipster is infallible; some of the recommendations may take far longer to mature than expected, while others may be outdated by the time the words reach the public.

Sometimes the writer is misled by poor reporting or is manipulated by press releases into picking out a stamp which later information shows to have been badly evaluated; this applies, of course, particularly to new and forthcoming issues. For this reason many tipsters stick to older stamps, where the market has had time to sort itself out and where unexpected changes are fewer. In such cases the quantities printed are known or can be estimated, the present popu-

larity of the country is known and its future can be more
easily assessed, and there is a sequence of previous catalogue and market quotations which can be examined before
making a judgment.

It is the tipster of new issues who takes his reputation
in his hands every time he writes—and it is his comments,
if sound, that are of the greatest value to the collector and
the investor. With such stamps the quantities may be unknown, and all the other factors may be conjectural: the
matter becomes a lot simpler if you understand what lies
behind the tipster's words.

One important point must never be forgotten by the
investor: the very act of tipping a stamp has an effect on
the market. The danger here lies in the undoubted fact that
mention by a reputable writer draws the investor's attention
to the issue, bringing extra demand for it and pushing up
the price. There are dealers who automatically buy additional
stocks of tipped stamps in the expectation of this demand,
and as a result some of these items may rise unnaturally
quickly, reach a pinnacle, and then decline slowly to a more
stable plateau from which they are very slow to rise again.
The investor who buys at top price may have to wait a
long time before he can realize a profit in such cases.

This is where your own expertise enters the picture: if
you can anticipate the rush and get in before the hottest
tips are broadcast to the public, you will have the advantage over everyone except possibly the wholesalers and
major dealers who will have large stocks of all issues. You
can place advance orders at new-issue prices—or, for older
stamps, at low current market prices—and then, in the case
of a speculated "flyer," can sell out speedily, before the
market wilts again.

How does one obtain the information to do this, and
how should such information be interpreted? For a start,
you will find that most magazines feature new-issue notes and
lists. These may give full details of the issue, with pictures,

values, quantities, colors, and much other data. These are fine as a check that you have not missed anything, but their compilation takes time and, with printing and block-making delays, the full listing may not appear for several months, long after the issue date and any price changes.

For the investor who likes to pick up extra sets of new issues at the best price, or who likes to dabble in occasional items outside his normal field if they look good to him, the real tool is the magazine's advance listing. This will be necessarily brief—it may give only the anticipated issue date (which may be changed several times before the stamps are released), the subject of the issue, and probably the face values of the stamps. Such advance information is invaluable if properly understood: here it is speed that counts.

> "New Caledonia. Future issues will include a 7f. for Stamp Day, showing a 19th century foot postman and thatched post office."

This quotation comes from a new-issue guide of June 1967. The stamp has not yet been a great investment success, but the theme—postal history portrayed on a stamp design— is perennially popular, and it is certain that the wide-awake collector who knew to make advance arrangements for his stamps, and perhaps a first-day cover, from a country which normally would not fall within his collecting field will have benefited from his foresight.

> "Belgium. On April the 2f., 3f. and 6f. definitives were issued on phosphorescent paper (sold in Brussels and Louvain regions only)."

The date was May 19, 1967, and the stamps had been on sale unannounced for a month. Few new-issue dealers would have supplied them on standing order, but bearing in mind what has happened to the early restricted-sale phosphor issues of Great Britain, this notice should have acted as an immediate signal to the investor. There is always a chance that such unannounced issues will have a very short life before being replaced by new designs, and the very lack of advance publicity is a good sign that most collectors will have missed out on them.

> "Great Britain. The 7d., 9d., and 10d. phosphor stamps are still on sale at the Philatelic Bureau, Edinburgh, in spite of some dealers having been informed that the 7d. was off sale. It is understood that the Bureau has at least a year's supply available."

The date was May 12, 1967, and a number of advertisements had appeared quoting higher prices for the "withdrawn" stamp. Here the news column helps the investor to avoid being panicked. Nevertheless, the stamps were scheduled for eventual withdrawal, so the collector should have made sure he got them, at face value, before it was too late.

> "Cook Islands. The £1, £3, and £5 New Zealand "Arms" postal-fiscals overprinted Cook Islands have been surcharged in decimal currency: $2, $6, and $10 respectively."

This was listed on July 14, 1967, and the report went on to state that quotas had been sharply cut and that odd quantities, in some cases very small, had been supplied, making it virtually impossible for dealers to supply sets. This, of course, was a little late in the day for action, but application direct to the islands by cable would probably have brought a few copies—and it was at least a tip to the keen investor that the sooner he telephoned every possible supplier the better it would be for him!

In this case, the small quantities available, together with the high cost of the stamps (a face value of $25.20 for the three), meant that few collectors got the set at all. Scott's catalogue quotes *no* price for these stamps, but present retail quotations are around $500 for the three—the moral here is obvious!

These are just a few brief examples chosen at random, with an attempt to ignore the more well-known flyers which could have been picked up cheaply as a result of keeping a keen eye on advance listings. The investor should maintain a permanent record of issues, orders, prices paid, and later market movements in these stamps. The time spent in producing such a record is well worthwhile; it will give invaluable pointers for future investments, while constant updating from the retail market advertisements provides a far safer check than any amount of haphazard scanning.

REGULAR STAMPS

AND OTHERS

STAMPS FALL INTO several categories according to the purpose of their issue, and each demands separate consideration as investments.

Regular stamps are, in North America, the normal issues of a country, used for ordinary postage and kept in use for a considerable length of time. It is important to note that in Britain and all other English-language countries these are called *definitives,* the word "regular" being considered too vague and apt to be confused with other meanings of the word, such as "regular" perforations or "regular" lines of shading on a design.

Regular stamps are intended to be permanently on sale in all post offices. However, policy considerations sometimes bring unexpected changes in the series in use, and occasionally a regular stamp will be abruptly withdrawn from use, or surcharged with a new face value, or replaced by a similar but slightly different version. Such short-lived regular stamps are very often overlooked by the average collector and even by dealers at the time, so that when at a later date the shortage of supplies is noticed these items see a speedy rise in value quite out of proportion to that for other stamps in the same range which have seen longer service.

The collector of U.S. stamps has a massive field for study

in that country's stamps alone, and it is for this reason that so many collectors do restrict themselves to these issues. From an investment viewpoint, however, such a course is fraught with pitfalls, for two reasons: there is little or no potential in most modern issues, and American collecting tends to embrace many labels which are in no sense *postal*.

Since the world market is restricted to *postal* stamps, markings, and services, the U.S. collector who invests in revenue stamps, Sanitary Fair labels, Christmas seals, or any other of the many fascinating items listed in Scott's Specialized United States Catalogue should do so in the absolute knowledge that the material he collects has little or no market anywhere except inside his own country. It is thus far more susceptible to fluctuation according to popularity and economic pressures than material with an international market.

Unexpected changes in U.S. regular stamps are uncommon, and since large stocks of all issues are usually taken up on issue there is little chance of profit here. In Great Britain, however, in the course of some fifteen years, regular stamps went through three entirely different watermarks, some values having sideways or inverted watermarks; there were also phosphor-lined and graphite-lined varieties (of which more later), booklet panes with se-tenant stamps and labels, different papers, and many noticeable shades. (Se-tenant refers to two or more stamps of different design or face value, or a stamp and a label, joined together by their perforations as sold by the post office.) A few printing errors added to the interest, and the stamps were printed in sheets bearing "cylinder numbers" indicating the printing cylinder from which they came, another specialist item for a collection! There were changes in postal rates, some reflected in the appearance and disappearance of certain values of the set. And all this in fifteen years to a set of some twenty basic stamps with a face value of about $1.40!

Whenever a change in the basic stamp is sufficiently important for it to merit a separate catalogue listing (and all those mentioned above did, with the exception of the paper types—and even these may well come to be listed later), there is a ready-made demand for it by every collector who buys stamps strictly according to the catalogue. At the same time, it must be remembered that collectors are on the whole creatures of habit, and a new departure in stamp production often leaves them cold until it is too late to jump on the bandwagon; thus the phosphor-lined issues of Great Britain were ignored for many years by the average collector, with the inevitable result that once the demand blossomed there just was not enough of the varieties to go around. So far as the commemoratives were concerned, this led to uninformed stockpiling at high prices by "investors" who knew just enough to get their fingers burnt—but that will be described later.

Reverting to our brief survey of the British regular stamps of the reign of Queen Elizabeth II as providing a textbook example of the sort of changes that affect regular issues of many countries, we find that in 1955 the original issue was superseded by a similar series but with the watermark changed from the original "Tudor Crown" to the "St. Edward's Crown." In 1958 this was again changed, to a simple "Multiple Crown" watermark, and toward the end of the use of this design some values appeared on unwatermarked paper.

A 4½d. value was added to the series in 1959, to cover changed postal rates. This was later withdrawn from sale when rates changed again, as was the 11d. value, which had appeared in the first two series but not on the "Multiple Crown" watermarked paper.

Booklets of stamps are printed in such a manner that, where watermarked paper is used, half the stamps are inverted in respect to the markings. Since booklet stamps are only a very small proportion of all stamps issued, and since in many cases the perforations at the edges are very badly cut (thus making the stamps unattractive to the collector), it can be seen that fine copies with inverted watermarks carry a sizable premium. Some booklets have the stamps stitched in sideways, and these therefore appear with the watermark either sideways or sideways-inverted.

Some values are also prepared for use in special stamp machines where the "feed" is sideways, rather than the bottom of the stamp coming from the machine as is the usual practice. These also have sideways watermarks in some cases, and are particularly scarce.

In 1957 a limited quantity of some values with graphite lines printed on the back was placed on sale in the town of Southampton; these were for use with automatic letter-facing machines which sorted the letters into order for machine postmarking by sensing the graphite content under the stamps. It was found that the machines were often confused by the printing on the envelopes, and this short-lived experiment was superseded by a new type of machine which detected phosphorescence instead. Stamps were then placed on sale with phosphor lines printed on the face, and these in the course of years went through several modifications, both in the numbers of lines found on certain values and in the type of phosphor-bearing compound used. Most of these varieties are of considerable value in comparison with the simple stamp on which they are found.

Here is a fine example of how a little study can provide many valuable finds for the collector. High values, which are simply the higher levels of the normal "regular" series, are often best considered separately. For U.S. stamps of recent years there is little or no difference in investment potential, but, looking again to Great Britain as an example of the general world-wide picture, you will find that certain stamps have improved quite amazingly over the past fifteen years.

British high values are the 2s.6d., 5s., 10s., and £1 values, which from 1955 to 1969 were in a double-size design, each showing a castle in England, Wales, Northern Ireland, or Scotland. These passed through several changes of printer, each imparting his own recognizable changes to the basic stamp, and through changes of watermark and, more noticeably than with the regular stamps, of paper. Phosphor and graphite lines are not found on these stamps.

Far too many British collectors were loath to part with 37s.6d. ($5.25) for this set of four of their own stamps, especially when there are so many cheap and attractive foreign stamps to acquire. Few dealers were prepared to tie up their money in such obvious slow movers, and many were caught unawares by each change that came along. Some of these changes were not even catalogued at first, so demand was negligible. A look at the current catalogue will show extremely high prices for these stamps which at the time were considered not worth bothering about.

It is almost axiomatic that in any country's stamps the high values will show a better rate of profit over a period than the lower ranges of the series, and this tendency was reinforced by the fact that until recent years most collectors took sets "to the shilling" (that is, they collected only the lower ranges of stamps). This was an early result of the increase in the flow of new issues; collectors preferred to keep as many countries going as they could rather than limit their scope to ensure completeness within certain countries. The tendency is now disappearing, but it has left its mark on the trade in past issues, and even today the high values of some smaller countries are automatically regarded as good property for this reason alone.

Provisional stamps are regular issues (or sometimes commemoratives pressed into regular service) which have been hurriedly overprinted or surcharged to fill unexpected gaps in postal supplies or to signal a change in the country's political complexion or in its currency. While one must take every provisional stamp on its own merits, there is no denying that their inherent short life and the chance of errors and varieties due to the speed of their production make them on the whole good investments.

We have already referred to the short-lived Cook Islands high-value decimal-currency surcharges; these were the tail end of a complete dual-currency series of surcharges bridging the gap between the suspension of sterling currency and the introduction of new decimal stamps. The entire series is well worth having, and the 2½¢ is particularly notable— alternate columns of the stamps have different forms of the figure ½, thus creating another major variety listed in Scott's catalogue.

At Mauke, a small island in the Cook group, the local postmaster took small quantities of the sterling stamps and hand-surcharged them in ball-point pen with the decimal equivalents. This, like the official issue, was designed both as a bridge until new stamps could be issued and as an educational exercise for the illiterate postal clerk, who had to accustom himself to the new currency. There are very few of the "Mauke hand-surcharges" in existence, and because of the obvious ease with which they could be imitated, they are acceptable only when postmarked with the Mauke handstamp between April and December 1967. These varieties are not listed in Scott's catalogues but are recognized by specialists in the field, and by virtue of their extreme scarcity would fetch very high prices within this specialist group.

In 1964 the sultan of Zanzibar was overthrown and a republic was declared. Stamps sold on January 14 of that year had the sultan's portrait cancelled by a manuscript cross, and copies so treated, with cancellations dated between January 14 and 17, are therefore of great interest. On the latter date a local handstamp, inscribed "Jamhuri 1964," came into use and this was applied to full sheets of stamps and also to single stamps on covers. By February 28 new supplies had arrived from England with a machine overprint, and these were then placed on sale. All these provisional issues are of value and when they first appeared caused quite an upset on the market, as nobody was sure of the quantities available.

Three of the 1960 Norfolk Island stamps previously discussed were provisional surcharges. Norfolk issues stamps only in the exact denominations required for current postal rates, so that increases in these rates brought surcharges on several stamps pending the production of new definitive stamps. The same thing is found on stamps of Papua–New Guinea and also of New Zealand and its dependencies, and these are almost invariably good investment property.

Another reason for provisional surcharges, now far less frequently encountered, is a temporary shortage of stamps of a particular value, necessitating the surcharging of other values as a stopgap. This practice was relatively common in some countries in the past, but has only rarely been seen in recent years; improved communications have lengthened the chances of even the most isolated country being without stamps for long. One recent example, however, is Ecuador. Because of an impoverished treasury, the government surcharged all sorts of older stamps rather than incur further bills for the production of new stamps.

An important factor to be borne in mind by the investor is that provisional surcharging often exhausts stocks of the basic stamp.

COMMEMORATIVES

AND THE REST

A STAMP ISSUED to mark an anniversary or other event is termed a *commemorative*. Pictorial stamps having no direct connection with such an occasion but which have a topical interest are correctly called *special stamps*, but the distinction is rarely made and, except so far as it may affect the period of issue or the popularity of a particular set, is of little importance to the investor.

Commemorative and special issues are limited in quantity and in period of sale; the figures may run from many millions, as in the case of most U.S. commemoratives, to only a few thousand stamps in the case of a small country. Because of the smaller quantities and limited issue period, market values tend to increase far more swiftly than those for regular stamps, but this aspect is also affected by fashion and by the overall popularity of the country and the theme portrayed.

A recent trend in commemorative stamps has been the "omnibus" series. One of the first omnibuses was that for the Silver Jubilee of King George V in 1935, when practically every country in the Commonwealth and Empire issued a set of stamps to mark the occasion. Those for the Crown Colonies were in an identical design, while the Dominions taking part had their own designs and some smaller countries merely overprinted regular stamps for the occasion. The series was a tremendous success with the collector, and dealers who had grossly underestimated the demand inundated the philatelic press with offers to buy any quantity. The series is still a textbook investment item despite recent hardening of the market, and first-day covers from almost every country are "blue chip" investments.

The accession of Edward VIII brought into being many extensive schemes by major dealers to provide full coverage of commemorative stamps for his coronation, and with his abdication the plans were transferred to the omnibus for the coronation of George VI in 1937. As a result, every collector and dealer overbought and the stamps became drugs on the market until quite recently, when increased capitalization brought tentative moves even here. The face value of the sets is low, stocks and even first-day covers for most issuing territories are ample at the moment, but no harm can come of putting aside a series for ultimate appreciation—although this is far from a red-hot tip!

The Peace issues of 1946 were also overbought, but when in 1948 the Royal Silver Wedding was honored by another omnibus the story was different. The occasion was thought by the postal authorities to merit the issue of not only a low-value stamp for inland postal service but also a high-value stamp from each territory, the face value of which varied from 5s. to £1 (70 cents to $2.80). The trade was up in arms at this attempt to, as they saw it, take the collector for a ride by releasing stamps for which in many cases there was no conceivable postal use. Many major dealers boycotted the high values, and investment in the colonial issues was very patchy.

It was the slow rise of the British Silver Wedding £1 stamp which heralded the rebirth of British stamps as investment material. After fifteen years of availability at face value (and even less in the trade), the price slowly climbed to $4, $7, and upward, so that today cylinder blocks and full sheets are quite desirable property. By that time, of course, most of the hapless investors of the late forties had disposed of their stocks at rock-bottom prices, and the stamp is a fine example of the dictum that every dog has its day.

In 1949 almost every country in the world joined with the British Commonwealth in producing stamps to mark the seventy-fifth anniversary of the Universal Postal Union. The investment progress of these issues has been patchy, but a close check of the quantities issued and the current market valuations will give a good guide to the future of any particular set. The centenary of the U.P.U. will be commemorated in 1974, and revived interest may well be forecast in these currently rather overlooked stamps.

The Crown Agents' release in 1963 of an omnibus issue for the Freedom from Hunger campaign was echoed by many other administrations, and this set enjoyed a reasonable popularity until a flood of other omnibuses, each bringing more tendentious and dull designs, rather sickened the public of the whole idea. Many of the later omnibuses include issues of smaller countries where quantities sold are exceptionally small, and while the future of the omnibus as a complete topic is in doubt, there is no denying that the astute collector can pick out many odd sets which are bound to provide a healthy investment.

In 1956 six European countries issued stamps of similar design to mark the concept of a United Europe. The following year two other countries joined in, and in 1960 the concept was allied with that of the nineteen-nation European Conference of Posts and Telecommunications; twenty countries issued stamps for the occasion and the "Europa" boom was on. Earlier issues came in ever greater demand, and the inclusion of British and Irish issues heightened European interest in other stamps of the two countries.

In 1961 Ireland dropped out, but since the annual conference was held at Torquay, Britain issued a second set. Fifteen other countries joined in, but the issues of Iceland and Turkey were heavily speculated and with the temporary impossibility of obtaining the Turkish stamps, many collectors throughout Europe became sick of the game and dropped out. The appearance of a speculative set from far-off Paraguay "in honor of Europa" did not help sweeten the taste, and with disillusion came a noticeable slowing down of the market.

Then 1962 brought eighteen new sets, plus a "tourist" issue from Albania prominently featuring the word "Europa." But the rot had set in, and soon large stocks of some of the more speculated countries began to appear on the market at much-reduced prices.

The annual omnibus still appears, but the craze has now died out and most investors consider them just a minor hazard in one-country collecting. Certain issues are well worth having, and in the long term all will turn out satisfactorily, but the investor is advised to exercise caution and concentrate only on those stamps on which he has detailed information as to quantities, demand, and probable future popularity.

The organized omnibus, then, is at least temporarily in eclipse. Other topics have perennial popularity, one of which is the "postal history" theme. A special group of these stamps is the "stamp on stamp" design: stamps of earlier days are reproduced on new issues which commemorate the centenary of the stamps or other occasion. There is a ready-made market for large quantities of any stamp-on-stamp issue, and it should be mentally filed away by any investor with an eye to dabbling outside his own specialty.

Other topics come and go; a recent favorite has been reproductions of paintings. The vast outpouring of these attractive stamps, aided by modern precision multicolor printing and the growth of private agencies providing unnecessary stamps for illiterate regions, may well kill the craze from a surfeit of good things, but many of these issues will achieve permanent "blue chip" status—mainly the earlier sets which were overlooked at the time of issue.

Typical of these are the French Arts stamps, the first of which appeared in 1961. The four stamps then issued were a mixture of designs, and the larger size of the stamps—essential for good reproduction of the original works of art—was deprecated by conservative collectors. Further stamps appeared piecemeal—three, then two, then two more, and then oddments—and slowly the first issues began to rise, not startlingly, but more swiftly than other French issues of the time. Suddenly the hunt was on, prices shot up, and now every new issue is snapped up in ever increasing quantities by collectors who do not seem to realize that the high prices for the earlier issues are a result of their relative scarcity in the face of increased demand and that a decrease in present demand would leave more copies of the recent issues on the market than it could easily absorb.

Such "extended issues"—sets which appear piecemeal over a period of years—are often susceptible to pressure in the same way. The Spanish Arms set is a good example, some odd values having become inordinately expensive, and the attractive Japanese Philatelic Week and International Letter-writing Week issues offer further confirmation. Here again is a pointer for the keen investor: Don't wait for an extended issue to become popular—get yours at the word go, then sit tight regardless of the comments of dealers or other collectors. Where an extended series seems to be well collected right from the start, as with the Spanish Costumes set, one might suggest taking up first-day covers and maximum cards as well.

An important factor in the investment potential of any commemorative set is the quantity printed and the period of time that the stamps remain on sale. British sets are usually available from the Philatelic Bureau for up to a year from the issue date, although in one startling case—the England Winners stamp issued in 1966 to mark the country's success in the World Football Cup Championship—the entire printing was exhausted almost overnight. The Post Office had announced in advance how many stamps would be available—somewhat in excess of 12 million—and this quantity seemed very low to the investor. (It is worth bearing in mind that this quantity was far higher than that of many higher-value phosphor-lined commemoratives which attained only a very slow rate of improvement at first.)

Often advance announcements trigger off similar panics for Crown Colony issues, and it is in the investor's interest to make arrangements as early as possible to avoid the rush, remembering that panic buying at the height of a temporary boom may be far more costly than waiting until the later plateau is reached. Genuine shortages, of course, will be reflected in future pricing regardless of any temporary panic.

A word of warning should be given about short-lived topical crazes, of which the Churchill omnibus provides a good example. When the first Churchill commemoratives appeared there was a genuine feeling of bereavement which moved collectors to purchase all issues as they came out. This was certainly encouraged by the very high standard of design of the U.S. stamp, a factor which will be dealt with later. However, the appearance of a number of speculative and manipulated agency issues put a damper on demand, especially when hapless buyers, tired of being milked, tried to dispose of their hasty purchases and discovered the lack of dealer interest in buying back the more blatant agency productions!

At present some of the Churchill stamps are very good property, especially in cases where the issuing country has a general popularity quite separate from any mere topical demand. The centenary of Churchill's birth occurs in 1974, and this may well bring further commemorative sets; if so, there will certainly be renewed demand for the earlier issues, but the investor should again be wary of purely speculative emissions.

"Permanent" topics are a different matter. Certainly fashions change; in the early days of flight, for example, any

airmail stamp was in tremendous demand, but this fell off
as air transportation became the usual means of carrying
long-range mails. Nonetheless, interest continues on a minor
scale, and any collection which contains a good selection of
early airmail stamps is certainly a valuable possession. One
could not, however, counsel the newcomer to tackle the field
at this late date, save within a small specialized collection
of a country where certain stamps and "first-flight" covers
may be an excellent investment.

More lasting topics are flowers, birds, and animals, and
the Red Cross and United Nations issues. The danger here
lies in overproduction, which has in fact already affected
all the topics mentioned: a recent catalogue of animal stamps
lists some four thousand different issues. The only solution
is to choose one category—sea birds, wild flowers of Europe,
reptiles, and so on—and develop a systematic collection in
this restricted field.

In any topical collection, much of its value will depend
on the amount of study and research the collector invests in
arranging and writing up his stamps logically. Topical collecting, therefore, is better followed by the collector with
an eye to future improvement than by the straightforward
investor who may not have the time or the interest to make
the most of his acquisitions. Certainly some topics are susceptible to investment purchase, but these are mainly very restricted groups with a fast turnover period.

Another branch of new issues is the *miniature sheet.*
This has an appeal all its own, and one which was rather
slow to catch on with the general collector. Basically, any
stamps which appear in a form other than that of the normal
post-office sheet are in miniature sheet format. However,
many such sheets bear no relevance to standard sheets but
are specially produced items containing one, two or three
se-tenant stamps with different designs, often imperforate,
which occur thus in no other form.

It is instructive to see what happened in Britain, where

Gibbons (publishers of the standard British catalogues) for many years refused to admit these items to their catalogues. A few canny collectors, however, swam against the stream—often a good thing to do where prejudice dictates the collecting habits of the majority—and built up collections comprised solely of miniature sheets. They are now reaping immense benefits from their daring and foresight.

To the purist, the miniature sheet is certainly suspect as being essentially non-postal (to apply the stamps to envelopes one has to cut up the sheet and throw the margins away) but they cannot be totally rejected since, despite their unwieldiness, they *can* be used to prepay postal charges, and that—and that alone—is the criterion of a postal emission. So by the time Gibbons recanted and admitted miniature sheets to their canon, the many issues unknown to most British collectors had forged ahead in America and Europe, where other catalogues were used. The British collector, precipitated into this raging torrent, threw himself and his cash about wildly in an attempt to catch up, and prices rocketed.

In most cases miniature sheets will continue to rise in value, at least in the foreseeable future, but any later revulsion from them as "collector bait"—which many of them are—would obviously have a bad effect on the market.

At present, American dealers are banned from importing the post-revolutionary issues of Cuba, North Korea, North Vietnam, and China. As a result, *all* the issues of these countries are rather low on the market (although stamps of Taiwan, inscribed "Republic of China," enjoy immense popularity thanks to excellent designs and careful publicity from the agency handling these issues). If the U.S. Government relents at some future date and the stamps are all admitted to catalogues and dealers' stocks, demand would inevitably grow and collectors would find themselves participating in a major market upheaval as prices spiraled upward.

Restricted conditions of sale affect the price of new

issues of some countries. In these cases, a limited quantity of imperforate stamps or miniature sheets, sometimes in altered colors, is produced; these are made available only to dealers who purchase correspondingly larger quantities of the normal issue. As can easily be seen, where the demand for a particular issue is 50,000 sets, and in order to acquire them the dealer has to buy 500,000 of the normal issue, the latter will be a drug on the market for many years. Alternatively, if he buys only 50,000 normal sets to fill his demand, he can acquire only 5,000 of the restricted items, which immediately have a scarcity value.

In either case, the situation is an artificial one, and the normal response of collectors is to distrust the guilty countries. Demand then falls off, surplus cheap stamps become even less likely to move, and the restricted sets also suffer. Dealers have learned to treat such countries with disdain, but there are always new collectors who think they know better. Any country which follows this practice is unlikely to be a worthwhile investment area until the philatelic policy of its administration is reformed. The sad thing is that when that happens, the earlier restricted issues tend to acquire an aura of respectability and prices start to rise again, to the annoyance of the collector who has quite rightly steered clear of them during the suspect period.

Other items which should be considered by the investor, and which do not fall into any of the major categories already discussed, are *officials* and *postage-dues*. These are not particularly popular with most collectors, mainly because they are relegated by most catalogues to subsidiary lists at the end of the major listing. They are, however, genuine postal issues, and those of many countries are well worth having, either fine-mint or properly used on covers. These will be discussed later along with other "sideline" material.

To sum up: the wise collector will subscribe to a comprehensive and reliable new-issue service; he will study closely the quantities and periods of sale of all short-lived

issues and keep up to date with all varieties of regular
stamps which merit or may in the future merit catalogue
status; he will make sure that he has all the high-value
stamps he can afford even before he bothers about the lower
ranges and will bear in mind the effect that particular topics,
omnibuses, and crazes may have on the market; he will
acquire a good understanding of the philatelic policy dictat-
ing a country's new issues and will carefully examine any
conditions of sale which attach to a particular issue.

But, of course, no collectors—and few investors—restrict
themselves to new issues. Older stamps offer a far wider
field for investment, a more interesting and better docu-
mented study for serious collecting—and considerable difficulty for the collector who aspires to completeness without
having the cash to buy them off the shelf. It is with this
fascinating study that we shall now deal.

BUYING

OLDER STAMPS

THE INVESTMENT potential of older stamps depends to a great extent on their past history. Previous crazes and prejudices are bound to affect catalogue quotations, and may well affect present demand and future prospects.

Western Australia at one time provided a popular field for many collectors, and catalogue valuations were conditioned by this demand. When popularity waned, the catalogued prices did not fall, since they reflected the buying prices at which major dealers' stocks were acquired and thus the selling price they hoped to obtain for them.

The smaller dealer, working with small quantities of stamps which have a constant turnover, can often offer slow lines at a discount, or even at a loss, to realize quick cash which he can then employ in a better field. The catalogue compiler is loath to let this affect his listings, partly because he knows that other dealers' prices are still high, and partly because drastic cuts are regarded by collectors as an unwarranted devaluation of their collections.

Before considering catalogue prices as a guide to purchase, the investor must always ask himself whether they reflect the current market. For some countries and some periods, 80 percent of catalogue price may be a fair retail price; for other stamps one may find it easy to buy at 50 percent or less. Then the question arises: Are stamps which are freely available at such a discount a good investment?

The answer to this depends on whether the catalogue prices have been inflated by past speculation or popularity, or whether the prices asked by the dealers are reduced because of a temporary lack of popularity which will soon pass—in which case, of course, the market price would then climb back to full catalogue price or even higher.

There is a slow but constant pendulum swing between catalogue price and market price. When the breach is wide, many collectors become disillusioned with their material and offer it for speedy sale at the best price they can get; this brings further unpopular material on the market and depresses the price still further. When a certain point is reached, junior collectors, attracted by the apparent bargains, start to acquire the cheaper items at large discounts and this demand may in time cause a slow upswing of retail prices, thus encouraging the investor to take part in the market again.

This is a long-term effect, but many quicker rises and falls occur through the influence of public popularity, particularly in the political field. The stamps of Nazi-occupied Europe serve as a good example; these were often not even reported in the American philatelic press at the time, and certainly no market price could be put on them, since they were not commercially available. As a result, some few issues attained a spurious scarcity value, but on the whole the issues were disdained by the patriotic populace. When prices finally settled down, they were usually far lower than similar issues of other countries would have been.

In the topical field one can cite the War Tax issues of World War I. These were immensely popular at the time of issue and for a short while after the war, but then enthusiasm waned in the postwar change of outlook and they are only now slowly recovering from their long neglect. In the twenties there was tremendous interest in what were called the "Neuropes"—issues of the new states founded as a result of the Treaty of Versailles and other postwar changes in Europe. These in turn suffered a slump, from which many have yet to recover.

It should not be thought that a country once damned is forever lost in a collector's no man's land. Philatelic crazes are odd things, and sooner or later every country seems to acquire popularity. The over-catalogued country comes into its own again and prices may even outreach previous highs, while the rejected and under-catalogued issues of the pariah countries suddenly acquire an interest in the public eye— stamps hitherto regarded as drugs on the market become sought after, stocks are found to have been depleted by the depredations of juniors over the years, and the race is on between cataloguer and dealer to surpass one another in raising prices in the face of the new demand.

Here is where the astute tipster must really have his ear to the ground. He must also have an encyclopedic knowledge of dealers' stocks, the history of the country's issues, the present and the probable future political situation there, and the possibility that a spurious and short-lived craze may be sparked off by a single large dealer with excess stocks to dispose of.

In recent years Italian dealers started wide-scale "investment drives," offering stamps at ever-increasing prices with an offer to repurchase later at a profit. Naturally for a time the lure was irresistible to the newly affluent Italians, especially as the stamps being speculated were earlier Italian issues with patriotic appeal. Soon, however, it became obvious that there were just too many stamps around for the dealers to be able to continue hedging their bets. Many issues slumped, but by that time the dealers had moved on to a new field—the Vatican.

Vatican issues have been produced in relatively minute printings, as befits a pocket principality, and these have a ready-made market among Catholic collectors throughout the world. The Italian dealers' investment drive was even

more successful here, and, of course, their appeal was to a
world-wide community and not solely to Italian collectors.
But in time there came a hiatus, and the dealers turned to
new pastures—and found San Marino.

San Marino, "the world's smallest republic," is a pocket
state buried in the heart of Italy. For many years its gaudy
issues of low values were a staple part of juniors' topical
packets; they are almost valueless. The high values of
these sets, in little demand, were printed in much smaller
quantities, and were treated with the same disdain that the
low values merited. But when the dealers built up a world-
wide publicity campaign, based on the "small printings"
of these gaudy labels, a horde of collectors allowed themselves to be hoodwinked into paying more and more for
them. In time all the available stocks were in the hands of
investors, the dealers had had their profit from them—and
suddenly nobody wanted to buy them any more.

These are a few of the pitfalls of buying older issues.
Stamps catalogued at premium prices may well still be
cheap at full catalogue price, if the country is due for a
rise as a whole. In other cases one-tenth catalogue may be
a foolish price to pay. On the other hand, if you can afford
to hold on long enough, even the dullest country may provide surprises—many the collector or investor who has tired
of holding on to his slow-moving material, has sold out at
a loss, and has then seen his dark horse emerge a few months
later and canter off to an easy win!

But in the purchase of older stamps the collector must
have a knowing eye for forgeries, fakes, and bogus issues,
or "album weeds," and these deserve separate discussion.

BEWARE OF

FORGERIES!

THE WORD "forgery" strictly means a complete fabrication of a stamp, cover, or other item which is intended to deceive; there are postal forgeries, philatelic forgeries, and facsimiles.

Postal forgeries are those made to defraud the postal administration—to be used as postage stamps with the aim of avoiding postal charges. There are not a great number of these, and in many cases they have acquired a high market value (often far higher than the genuine stamps which they imitate).

The first postal forgeries were officially made by the British Post Office, to find out just how easy it would be for the forger to defraud them. Later examples come from France, Australia, and other countries, and behind many of the stamps are fascinating stories explaining their manufacture. Occasionally postal forgeries are found among old dealer stocks or in old collections where they have lain unrecognized for years, and it is certainly in the collector's interest to know all about those of his own specialty.

A special branch of postal forgery is the propaganda forgery; this is intended not only to mislead the postal authorities but also to bring home a propaganda point to the recipient of the letter. Both Germany and the United States made such items during World War II, and the Communist authorities in North Korea are currently feeding material into the world's mails franked with similar items. The history of this interesting branch of philatelic study goes back at least to the World War I period.

Philatelic forgeries are a real danger to the collector. These are fabrications prepared to swindle collectors, and many specialist books exist giving details of them. Forgeries of early and valuable stamps are, of course, the most common, but forged overprints on cheaper stamps are well known, and in recent years forged postmarks have been produced to enhance the value of stamps and covers. Luckily, forgeries of recent issues are rarely encountered, but modern multicolor printing processes are now so refined that, rather than printing stamps themselves, many small countries and agencies entrust the job to printers who lack proper security supervision, and it is therefore to be feared that contrived errors and reprints may appear on the market in years to come which may be indistinguishable from the genuine article.

Expert Committees exist which will authenticate stamps for a fee, and the collector is counseled to make use of their services whenever he is offered old or rare stamps without certificates.

Facsimiles have a long and disreputable history. In the early days of collecting, when the aim was simply to fill the spaces in a printed album, many collectors happily bought imitations of rare stamps and mounted them knowing that they were not genuine. Later purchasers of these collections may have been misled—but not for long! The facsimiles were sold at a small fraction of the normal price, and they satisfied the mania, in those early and naïve days, for sheer acquisition and completeness. Some, however, are well executed and may easily deceive the newcomer.

Fakes are genuine stamps which have been altered in some way so as to "improve" their value. It is here that real danger exists for the neophyte, and even the expert can be fooled occasionally. The simplest form of fake is the repaired stamp: torn, creased, or cut stamps, thinned or heavily postmarked, fiscally used or otherwise discounted copies can be cleaned up and made more presentable with a view to deceiving the purchaser.

As the art of the faker improves, so the experts must keep one step ahead, and many a stamp long cherished by its owner has been discarded in later years when it comes under expert scrutiny.

Remember that any stamp which has been "doctored" in this way is a bad buy. No matter how skillful the repair, it is a spoiled item and will never attain to great value. The rarest stamp in the world, the British Guiana 1¢ black-on-magenta of 1856, is in an almost unbearably tatty condition, badly stained and with its corners gone—yet only a vandal would suggest repairing it.

To clean or iron a stamp to improve its appearance is justified, and even more so with covers, where judicious cutting and splicing will restore a tatty cover without affecting its postal interest or value. But to remove a fiscal cancellation, to add rare postmarks to a cover or stamp, to add margins or perforations to a damaged stamp or to pad out thin spots is to resort to trickery in an attempt to make something what it is not.

A special warning here to the collector of "mint-unmounted" stamps: with the exception of low-value U.S. commemoratives overbought by investors, few copies of stamps more than thirty years old can exist in pristine mint condition, unless they are in sheets or panes, which are, of course, exceptionally scarce for most better stamps. This explains the vastly higher prices which fine-unmounted copies often demand. But the addition of gum to a mounted stamp is a matter of relative simplicity, and many firms now exist, particularly in Europe, which will supply the unscrupulous dealer or collector with regummed stamps—even going so far as to destroy three poor copies of a particular stamp to take from them the gum needed to provide one copy with full original gum. Be assured that such faking will in time become recognizable to the expert. Unless you know the full history of a rare stamp, do not accept its full gum "at face value."

Remainders are not in any sense forgeries, nor are *reprints*. In the study of these, a fine example is found in Scott's listing of the Samoa "Express" stamps. After the service was discontinued, large stocks of the stamps were found in sheets of twenty-one stamps (unlike the issued ones, which were in sheets of ten or twenty), including a 2d. rose value which was never actually issued in any form. These remainders, officially printed and prepared for use, were sold off to dealers at the time. In later years reprints were made in sheets of forty stamps, from the original plates used to produce the stamps; these also were sold to the trade. Neither was *used* for postage, since the service was closed down, but where the former had been prepared for use, the latter were made purely for the collector.

The picture is complicated by three entirely different forgeries prepared at different times by different hands, one quite dangerous, the others easily distinguished. In recent years facsimiles, with the word "Reprint" printed on the back (incorrectly, as we have seen), have appeared in junior approval selections. All in all, these Samoan stamps provide a marvelous training for any newcomer to the field of forgery detection!

GETTING THE

BACKGROUND

Do NOT DEPEND solely on the tipster to give you the background of older stamps in your field or to advise you on their prospects. Every country has a following somewhere in the world, and there are many specialist societies where collectors with shared enthusiasms can get together, if only by correspondence.

Societies publish invaluable bulletins which provide new issue notes, background information and studies of older issues, and specialized information on postal history, cancellations, and the other aspects of advanced collecting. Join a society—the subscription fee will be saved over and over by what you learn (even if at first much of the bulletin is way over your head). Not only will study guide you against making bad purchases, but it will put you in the way of good material and open your eyes to many fine bargains which lie unrecognized in dealers' stocks and auction lots.

Don't waste time working over old ground all by yourself. During the past thirty years the specialist societies, through books, monographs, and articles in the general and philatelic press, have made available the results of all the greatest collectors' studies. Philatelic bibliography—keeping a record of all that has been written—has become almost a study in itself. The society will help the newcomer in tracking down the facts he needs.

In collecting old stamps, the investor must pay particular attention to quantities and use. If the greater part of a stamp issue has been used up by an isolated people on local letters, then fine-mint copies will be at a considerable premium and even used copies will be scarce, as the recipients will have thrown them away without thought of their future value. But where a country has supplied the greater part of its stamp issues direct to the trade in mint condition, then fine-used copies will be at a premium and genuine local covers may be quite scarce.

A country with a large overseas mail, such as India or Australia, will provide the collector with plentiful covers of any period. High-value stamps will be easier to acquire postally used, for overseas mail demands higher postage rates, and where goods of considerable value are exported by mail, registry and insurance charges will increase the face value of the stamps used. When this point is reached—as with the £2 and £5 values of New Guinea issued in 1935—then mint stamps will be scarcer than used ones, since few collectors or dealers would have been prepared to tie up such large sums in single stamps; in this particular case, insured parcels sent from the gold fields ensured that a fair number of these stamps were postally used.

On the other hand, in many countries very high value stamps may well have served only fiscal use, although they may be inscribed "Postage & Revenue." In some cases the stamps are not listed in Scott's catalogue and so realize prices far lower, mint or used, than their original face value—another example of how the catalogue dictates public taste and controls the market.

As to quantities: broadly speaking, any stamp with a printing of, say, 10,000 copies will demand a higher price than one from the same country and period with a printing of 100,000. But the rule is more honored in the breach, and taste seems to enter very strongly into the picture, as well as postal use, purpose of issue, and other random factors.

However, in recent years printing quantities have come to be scrutinized more carefully than before, both by collectors and by the cataloguers, and any collector should make sure he possesses all the stamps with very limited printings, regardless of whether the catalogue or market price seems to bear out this advice. Bearing in mind the *use* of such stamps, in time they will assuredly attain the promise inherent in their relative scarcity.

The next thing the aspiring specialist will have to consider—and very carefully indeed—is the study of varieties and flaws. Technical philately has always leaned very heavily on the minute study of individual stamps, their examination in strips and blocks and, if available, in full sheets. The aim of such study is to identify each stamp's position on each printing plate so that any individual stamp can be allocated to its place—this is known as "plating"—and to chronicle flaws and damage to the plate during the printing runs that affected the stamps.

Nowadays, when full sheets of all new issues are available to the collector from any good dealer, such studies are falling into disuse. In modern methods of stamp production there is far less variation in individual stamps, while the photogravure process produces a vast number of minor and transient varieties of no philatelic interest whatsoever.

But old habits die hard, and there are still today many collectors who buy full sheets of new stamps and categorize the minor and major varieties which occur. Their task is far easier than that of the old-time collector, who had neither the full sheets nor the technical aids available to him, and it is certain that such study will continue to hold a tremendous attraction for a certain type of collector.

Always remember that many older stamps were produced under conditions which today would be regarded as primitive. Major errors in the paper used, in perforation, ink, and impression, and casual damage to the printing plates were far more common than today. The detection of such varieties made a genuine addition to philatelic knowledge, enabling the collector to build up a more complete and meaningful display of a country's stamps and to acquire as "normals" many stamps which by virtue of their relative scarcity as varieties would later come to acquire high premium value.

Catalogues play a very important part here. A catalogued variety has a "pedigree" and becomes sought after; an uncatalogued error or variety is suspect to the average collector, who prefers to play safe and follow the book rather than risk paying a higher price for something not yet recognized by his mentors. But catalogues are becoming more and more specialized. The collector of U.S. issues is well served by Scott's Specialized United States Catalogue, which provides extremely detailed priced listings of all the stamps mint, used, on first-day covers, in blocks of four, and in plate-number blocks, and very often it prices scarcer postmarks, especially on older issues. Printing quantities are given, postal stationery is dealt with in detail, and all the sideline interests of the U.S. collector—revenue stamps from playing cards and hunting permits, Sanitary Fair labels, postage currency items, and a wealth of other non-postal material—are carefully catalogued and illustrated.

This is a very patchy development, however. Stamps of Hungary or Afghanistan with relatively important varieties are virtually unsalable except in the country of origin or to a fellow specialist, while quite minor flaws on U.S., French, and British stamps have a recognized world-wide market. There is certainly scope here for investment, since it is impossible to predict which countries will be the next to come into the public eye, with consequent greater interest in varieties.

The important thing to remember is that having got your flaws and varieties, you must *do* something with them. Merely to fill a few albums with faulty stamps, each with its adhesive arrow indicating the point of variety, is to contribute nothing to the study. But to discover how and why the faults occurred, to trace their development and the effect it may have had on the issue as a whole, is true philately.

Regardless of the country studied, a collection of flaws and varieties will always command a premium over a simple collection of normal stamps. If in time you become an original expert in your chosen field, you may then compile your own specialist catalogue—and the world will then walk in *your* footsteps.

It is of paramount importance to distinguish between errors, varieties, constant flaws, and nonconstant flaws. An *error* is a definite mistake which may be found on one stamp in a regular position on a sheet or on every stamp; examples of this are the inscription "Walter Lily" found on the first printing of the Cook Islands 1967 4¢ stamp in mistake for "Water Lily," and the reversed "Z" found on the 6¢ Newfoundland stamp of 1910.

A *variety* is any stamp which differs from others of the same major type. The word is very broadly used and misused: changes of watermark or perforation, of color or shade, are all referred to as varieties and, in all but the most simplified catalogues, are usually catalogued as though the variants were separate issues. Such changes are nowadays usually announced by the postal administration in advance of issue, although occasionally they occur on only a small percentage of a printing as the result of a mechanical breakdown. A fine example of this was the issue of decimally overprinted "Arms" stamps for Niue (a New Zealand dependency) in 1967. A small quantity of sheets were released with variant perforations due to breakdown and the substitute use of two antique machines, and several major shades exist from different original printings of the basic stamps overprinted.

Such varieties are listed in specialist catalogues at first, and often later come to be shown in all the standard cata-

logues. In the Niue case the facts were made known at an
early date and were corroborated by the postal administration after the event, but in many cases no comment is forthcoming from the authorities and the philatelic detective
comes into his own. Naturally such investigation was far
more necessary—but far more difficult—in the past.

A glance at the catalogue will show the advantage of
making certain of such major varieties as the Niue perforation changes at point of issue and not leaving their acquisition to chance!

Constant flaws are marks on stamps caused by minor
faults in the preparation of the printing plates or by damage
to the plates during use. Attempts are often made to correct or disguise such flaws either before or during the printing run and these may produce *retouches,* which are distinguishable from both the normal stamp and the original
flaw. Such flaws have value according to their importance
and size, to the oddities which they may produce, such as
a mustache on the queen's portrait, and to the degree of
specialization acceptable to collectors interested in the country concerned.

Nonconstant flaws are those caused by temporary inter-
ference with the normal production of the stamps. They may
include such major errors as missing colors in multicolor designs or missing rows of perforation, in which case the
stamps will have a high market value regardless of their
philatelic insignificance; or they may involve merely specks
or white spaces on part of the design, creases across the
stamp, or the circular "ring flaws" often found on litho-
graphed stamps printed in tropical countries where dirt
adheres to the printing plate and disturbs the ink. Thin
white scratchmarks across the design may be caused by dirt
adhering to the "doctor blade," which wipes clean the photogravure printing cylinder, and, of course, minor misplace-
ments of color giving blurred or double impressions in multicolor printing also come under this category.

Nonconstant flaws have no real importance, and although high prices are often asked for them the collector is advised *not* to spend a lot on such items. If you acquire them at face value across the post-office counter, the best advice is to dispose of them straightaway for as high a figure as possible and use the proceeds to fill some real gaps in your collection.

POSTAL

HISTORY

THE APOCRYPHAL STORY of two brother collectors has been told many times but surely deserves retelling here.

The two brothers, Jim and Bill, lived in London toward the end of the last century. Both were collectors, but while Jim was a philatelist of the old school, methodical and painstaking, Bill "hadn't the time" to arrange his collection. Jim carefully soaked his stamps, mounted them with the heavy hinges then available, classified them according to the catalogue, and sold off his duplicates. Bill hoarded every cover that came his way; they went into shoeboxes and cupboards, roughly sorted by countries and dates, with duplicate stamps galore—just as he received them through the mail or from his friends. Both got great pleasure from the hobby, but neither could understand the other.

In time the two brothers died and their collections were turned over to reputable dealers for valuation. Jim's collection was speedily and accurately dealt with: the albums were well cared for, the stamps were all nice clean copies with light cancellations, and there was a respectable showing of rarer stamps and varieties, all annotated and properly arranged. A good price was realized at auction, the stamps being offered country by country with full descriptions of the "plums." But almost invariably the comment was, "Heavily mounted but typical of the period."

When Bill's haphazard accumulation arrived at the auction rooms the describers winced. But they got down to sorting through the covers and their eyes popped:

"Look at this cancellation—and the transit markings!"

"And this is probably unique—I never saw this cancellation before on a cover."

"And here's one that shows that mail from such-and-such went via so-and-so during that period—here's the additional franking rate for overland transit."

"Look at this—and this . . ."

The auction was a sensation, with dealers and collectors competing for material from all countries and periods. Prices were unprecedented, and all agreed that Bill, by his careful storage of complete sequences of correspondence in such fine condition (for hoarder though he was, Bill was no fool and cherished his material) had enriched the world's stock of postal-history material more than any other source in the past ten years!

One moral from this story is, of course, that tastes change. Postal history, the study of the postage stamp in the context of the postal service as a whole and not merely as a printed label in its own right, has totally changed the whole face of philately. But there is a second moral: Bill had really cared for his covers; he had been lucky in his correspondents, who had been at the right places at the right time; he had kept careful records of each contact, and his covers told a story of the development of postal services in a variety of countries, with graphic examples backed up by authentic background information culled from the letters themselves.

There is a final thought, just to keep the record straight: Jim's collection might have contained items unique in "straight" philately, while Bill's accumulation might well have offered nothing but common stamps with common postmarks!

The criterion of a postal-history collection lies basically in its ability to tell a story, the story of the mails. Certainly it may include single unique items of great value; on the other hand, one can build up a complete "reference collection" of covers, showing every possible postmark and every combination of routes, which will, from both the interest angle and the investment viewpoint, contain a tremendous amount of "dead wood"—just like a straight stamp collection.

The same criteria of popularity and scarcity apply to covers as to stamps. Nowadays it is no great task to assemble, through placing a single order with the Philatelic Bureau of the country, a collection of covers showing every current postmark of the post offices of Samoa or the Gilbert and Ellice Islands. But to obtain even a single example of the postmark of some of the same isolated offices dating from, say, forty years back, one may be involved in not only an expensive purchase but a lengthy and costly search for the item.

Even modern postmarks may turn out to be scarce. Mangaia, in the Cook Islands, has had a post office since about 1892, and early examples of its marks are scarce. But in 1963 the current datestamp was damaged and a temporary "relief" skeleton handstamp was brought into use from March 1 to April 27 of that year only. I need hardly comment on the scarcity and value of this postmark used on cover!

There are a number of specialized collectors interested in the postal markings of the Cook Islands, and all will vie to have one of the few examples in their collection. Such items, like the "Mauke hand-surcharges" on cover, just are not plentiful enough to go around—and this sums up the entire investment potential of postal-history material in recent years.

There are many specialized books and articles on the subject of early pre-stamp postal markings—the handstamps applied to letters in the days before the invention of the adhesive to indicate the postal charges. The novice is cautioned against thinking that *any* pre-stamp marking is valuable: many are far more common than the scarcer modern postmarks. Again study is necessary and again I say: Join a specialist society.

One of the most attractive things about postal-history collecting for the investor and the collector is the fact that little has really been worked out in comparative values. There are books which purport to give a "points value" for particular marks, but there is no hard-and-fast rule for calculating the real value of multiple markings and stamps on any particular cover. Of course, the condition of a cover is important, but less so than for stamps—and a cover may well be worth thousands of dollars even with a damaged stamp on it. Also, one can clean up covers more safely than stamps.

A word on the care of covers: modern papers often contain chemicals inimical to long life, and may damage the stamps stuck on them or even contaminate other covers stored with them. Older covers are on the whole more stable, but even here the interaction of paper and inks may bring difficulty. Competent chemical advice should be sought before you try to treat any staining or damage, or you may well ruin the item completely.

Fortunately, even in the earlier days of philately there were a few wise collectors who realized the possible value of postmarks. A few of these, finding that they could not rely solely on casual acquisitions or on personal correspondence to supply them with all the markings that existed, prepared self-addressed covers and sent them to far-off towns and islands for cancellation and return. Many postal administrations, particularly in Britain and the colonies, frowned on this practice and refused to postmark covers sent to them in this way, some going so far as to return covers with a letter stating their inability to perform the service requested —the cover being enclosed in an official envelope bearing just the postmark required!

A quantity of these prepared covers exists, thanks to the

foresight of these early collectors, and without them there is no doubt that many markings might otherwise never have been known to the collector. We owe a great debt to the few enthusiasts who went to such lengths, and although purists may sneer at "philatelically prepared" covers many have an honorable place in any collection today.

The practice has been kept up to the present day, and few collections of the modern postal markings of Barakoma, in the Solomon Islands, or the smaller offices of Papua and New Guinea are without a sprinkling of covers addressed to the Rev. Harry Voyce. A "BCM" address turns up again and again on covers bearing scarcer ship markings of modern times, and the name Roger Wells is seen on Pacific Island covers over many years. Certainly such material has a lesser value than genuine commercial mail bearing the same markings—but how and where can such mail be obtained?

To sum up briefly: there is still much to be learned about postal history, and there is tremendous scope for even the newcomer to make a significant contribution to our knowledge. In the absence of detailed priced catalogues, the value of a scarce cover is often a matter for haggling, and this means that the experienced collector has the chance to pick up rare items at a fraction of their real value. There is a handful of dealers who have the expertise to make fairly accurate valuations, but the field is so vast that no man can hope to know all the answers. Postal history is certainly one of the great investment fields of the future, and can be recommended without reservation to any collector who is prepared to put in the study necessary to recognize a good thing when he sees it.

1

2

3

4

A QUESTION OF VALUE

Never take a stamp for granted! This common U.S. 2¢ stamp (1) was printed by several methods and exists in different types; your copy may have a value of 10¢ or $50 or more according to its type, so it pays you to find out all you can about such varieties.

The 24¢ airmail error (2), depicting "Jenny" looping the loop, now fetches anything from $30,000 upward when occasional copies appear on the market, while attractive stamps like the others above (3,4) are valued today in pennies. The reason for these discrepancies lies, of course, in the quantity of each stamp available.

5

7

6

8

UNITED STATES FAVORITES

American collectors, naturally enough, tend to concentrate on stamps closely connected with the United States. The attractive issues of the United Nations at Lake Success (5, 6) have an international popularity which absorbs vast quantities of the stamps despite their very restricted actual postal use, while current interest in the entire Pacific Ocean area makes Hawaii's stamps a good investment—even completely bogus items (7) are sought after and demand high prices.

U.S. involvement in the Ryukyu Islands has brought considerable rises, particularly in the scarce earlier stamps (8), and the short-lived but historic issues of the Confederate States have a permanent popularity (9).

9

10

12

13

11

14

THE HOME OF THE POSTAGE STAMP

Great Britain issued the world's first adhesive postage stamp, the famous Penny Black (10), in 1840; it has been the subject of intensive study ever since and is one of the blue chips of philately. An "Official" stamp with the letters "VR" in the top corners (11) was prepared for use but never issued; despite this lack of recognition, copies demand very high prices and this fine pair would excite immense interest if offered for sale by auction.

It was the slow but steady rise in market price for the £1 Silver Wedding (12) stamp that signalized the beginning of the recent boom in British stamps; on the other hand, the World Football Cup Winners stamp (13) provides a textbook example of uninformed speculation and a warning to every investor.

Combining two popular topics—Christmas stamps and paintings on stamps—this 1967 stamp (14) exists in too large quantities to make it a worthwhile investment.

74

15

17

16

18

AROUND THE COMMONWEALTH

There is immense scope for collectors among the stamps of the British Commonwealth. Map stamps (15) are always popular, and this one has the added interest of depicting the Antarctic, a promising area for future development.

Maori art makes an unusual subject for study; this New Zealand stamp (16) is just one of many in the field. Another attractive topic, and one with an international following, is nudes on stamps (17), a topic for which a detailed checklist has been prepared by the American Topical Association.

Less promising, however, are gimmicks such as the Gold Coin issue of Tonga (18); die-stamped on metal foil and actually 3⅛ inches in diameter, these rose rapidly in price when they first appeared, because of demand from coin collectors, but soon settled down at a much lower level as collectors came to realize their speculative nature.

75

19

20

21

LOOK FOR THE MISTAKES

Major errors often create considerable interest, depending on the popularity of the country and the remarkability of the mistake. Faulty printing produced this unique block of surcharged stamps from Kuwait (19)—a real exhibition piece.

For many years it was believed that this Western Australia stamp (20) had an "Inverted Swan." Subsequent research proved it was the frame which was upside down, but this perennially popular variety still bears the (wrong) name and also carries a price tag around $6,500.

The arrow on the Tanganyika stamp (21) indicates a missing "1" in the dateline. A rare and quite valuable item, this is one of which copies may still exist unrecognized in collections, making a worthwhile reward for the watchful collector.

22

24

23

IN SEARCH OF THE UNUSUAL

Many collectors are scared off Asian stamps by their incomprehensible languages and strange designs; certainly care should be exercised in choosing a country for study, but there is much of interest—and a real chance for profit—in these exotic issues.

Be warned about stamps like this one, purporting to come from the South Moluccas (22); these are one of the traps of postwar philately. None was ever postally used, and none deserves to be regarded as a postage stamp. Yet they still turn up in collections!

Laos has always had a following in the United States; its stamps are both colorful and well designed. The item illustrated (23) is the top value of a set marking the King's Jubilee, and is one of the most valuable stamps of this Oriental kingdom.

Nepal is a country which has never had a strong following; its stamps are on the whole ill-produced and unattractive to the Western eye, but this situation is changing and many of the earlier stamps—and even quite recent ones like this 1958 airmail stamp (24)—may in time come to demand higher prices by virtue of the extremely small printing quantities.

25

27

28

26

29

ECHOES OF THE NAZI JACKBOOT

Germany offers tremendous scope for the student of propaganda on stamps, ranging from the Old German States through the first Reich to the Weimar Republic, the Nazi period, and the breakup of the country into East and West.

The stamps above come from the Nazi era; at time of issue they were snapped up by German collectors, but after the war suffered an eclipse from which they are now recovering. The German Eagle (25) enfolds the town of Nuremberg—an excellent example of the quality of design at this time, while a finely posed portrait of a Hitler Youth (26) depicts the strength of the Nazi idea on young minds.

The National Labor Day issue of 1939 (27) carries a high "charity" surcharge of 19pf. on a stamp whose franking power was only 6pf.; such a high charge would today incur the condemnation of the F.I.P. and, as it discouraged collectors at the time from stock-piling copies, the stamp has improved considerably in value.

This 6pf. stamp (28) is an example of one where a low-value issue has increased more in value than the higher value of the same set, due entirely to the relative quantity of copies now in existence.

Hitler's slow swallowing of surrounding territories was often marked by special stamp issues; this one commemorating his acquisition of the Sudetenland (29) is a milestone in a process which led to World War II.

30

33

31

32

34

ANTI-NAZI PROPAGANDA

After the excess of Nazi nationalism came a swing to the other extreme with the communization of the East. However, the first stamp illustrated here (30) dates from the war years; it is an illicit Allied propaganda item based on a genuine Nazi stamp, and shows a Gestapo man crouching menacingly behind a manacled prisoner; needless to say, Hitler's "Culture Fund" did not benefit from the 8pf. surcharge shown here!

One of the East German stamps issued for the International Geophysical Year depicted a Russian Sputnik (31) with the date of launching of this first artificial satellite. Mao Tse-tung appeared on this 1951 stamp (32) to honor German-Chinese friendship—hardly a likely theme today! On several occasions East Germany has issued stamps in remembrance of the Nazi holocaust, and the one illustrated (33) carries a large surcharge which was devoted to the construction of a national memorial at Buchenwald. Similar stamps have not been forthcoming from West Germany.

In common with other Communist satellites, East Germany issued a stamp (34) marking the first anniversary of Stalin's death. It is interesting to consider the Germans' attitude toward the late dictator ten years earlier— and only a few years later!

35

37

36

38

FRANCE: A PROUD NATION

One noticeable aspect of French stamp design is its stress on purely national pride, but this has now been widened to include the country's position in United Europe. Always á popular country with collectors and investors, these stamps illustrate a few of the many attractions of France.

First, the European concept is embodied in the annual Europa issue (35); these are popular throughout western Europe, but it is the earlier issues which on the whole have shown the best improvement.

"The Imaginary Museum" is the title of an extended series of attractive large-format stamps issued at intervals since 1961 (36); paintings, bas-reliefs, stained glass windows and other treasures have been featured on these stamps, and as is the case with most extended series the earlier issues now demand considerable premiums.

A more recent extended series is the "Great Names in French History" (37), which will in time cover the whole period of French history. Less popular outside the issuing country, these are nonetheless worth taking up for future profit.

Stamps of the Council of Europe (38) are valid for use only from the Council building in Strasbourg; they have a small but faithful following, particularly among collectors of United Nations stamps, and again portray France's position in Europe.

39

42

41

40

43

TOPICAL FRENCH ISSUES

The Battle of Hastings, which brought Norman-French rule to Britain and so led to the world of Western democracy we know today, was commemorated on an attractive stamp (39) which falls into many topical areas. The architectural glories of the country are portrayed on many "Tourist" issues (40); by now one could probably find stamps depicting scenes from every city in France, and most are of a very high level of design which makes them popular throughout the world.

Another popular topic, heraldry, has been immensely enriched by the many small-arms stamps (41) which have appeared piecemeal over the years; few of these are costly—unlike the Tourist issues, which contain some extremely valuable items—and they make a most attractive display.

Considerable consternation was expressed outside France when this airmail stamp (42) appeared in 1947, but it is now universally accepted and adds another example to the nudes on stamps topic.

New collectors are sometimes confused by the inscription "France Libre" which appears on many French colonial stamps (43); this was applied during the war to indicate the colony's adherence to General de Gaulle's "Free French" appeal, and so plays a part in telling the story of France's struggle against the Nazis.

45

46

44

FROM AFRICA TO THE ANTARCTIC

French colonial power has encompassed many lands, and the stamp issues of these countries provide immense scope for collectors. The large piece here (44) bears a high-value airmail stamp of Madagascar (in the Indian Ocean) overprinted for use in Terre Adelie—part of the French sphere of interest in the Antarctic. The stamp itself already has a good market value, but this is enhanced here by its being affixed to a cover bearing the special cancellation for the opening of the French postal service to this frozen outpost, and the datestamp of the first post office there.

From French West Africa comes this typical example (45) of the many stamps depicting local inhabitants and their customs. These attractive stamps were at one time a mainstay of junior packets of cheap stamps, but with the passage of time many have come to acquire quite respectable values!

A country having what must be among the world's most oddball designs is Tunisia (46); this intriguing design by Gandon is typical of the country's strange appeal, which may in time lead to a noticeable growth in international popularity.

47

48

49

THE LURE OF THE EAST

Egypt, Israel and Japan typify three different approaches to stamp design, yet all are attractive and each has its own following among collectors.

Pharaonic dress is shown on this Post Day issue (47); although Egypt is not in the forefront of investment collecting, stamps such as this should do much to enlarge its appeal.

The Israeli stamp (48) is one of a series issued for the 1965 New Year celebrations, and tells a part of the story of the creation of the world. It would be hard to imagine a more simple evocation of the words "Let there be light," and the "tab" at the foot of this rather odd-shaped stamp bears in Hebrew and French the inscription "The Creation—First Day," thus freeing the actual stamp design for clearer placing of the country name in three languages and the words "Joyous Festivals" which appear on all New Year stamps.

The flying geese on this delightful Japanese stamp (49) are based on a painting by Hiroshige; the second of a series marking Philatelic Week, its tasteful design makes it attractive to most collectors, while the small printing quantity endears it to investors. Recent Japanese issues have appeared in larger quantities and so have less investment potential, but all share the individual approach to stamp design which makes their collection a never-ending pleasure.

50

51

PROMISING SIDELINES

Depending on what countries you collect, you will find sideline items such as those illustrated here: U.P.U. "Specimen" overprints (50), and postage-dues (51).

These are genuine postal items and are well worth the collector's especial attention, particularly since they tend to be overlooked by many.

However, you should be careful to distinguish between these and, for example, "Specimen" overprints which have no connection with the Universal Postal Union. These, though of interest, cannot have the same investment potential.

53

52

UNPOPULAR COUNTRIES

It often pays to get right off the beaten track and to take up some countries which are currently ignored by collectors.

The two stamps illustrated above are examples of this; they are from St. Thomas & Principe (52), a tiny Portuguese colony off the west coast of Africa, and Morocco (53), a kingdom in North Africa which has used stamps of Britain, France and Spain in the past as well as having its own local posts, but which has been currently unpopular.

The lack of demand for such stamps means you may pick up copies— or even large selections—very cheaply. Your own individual study can turn such material into a fascinating collection and one which in time may come to demand a very high price.

54

55

THE MORE YOU LEARN . . .

A common British stamp (54) provides you with far more than you would imagine: varieties of watermark type and position, paper, shade and postal use mean that a good display could be constructed from careful study of this simple stamp, and already there are some scarcities among the varieties. The Turkish stamp (55) is made immeasurably more valuable by its postmark, since it proves its use in what is now a town of Israel; "Holy Land philately" is universally popular and material of this type is scarce.

Finally, there are several stamps which are occasionally found with inverted watermarks, and these aways carry a substantial premium. So it pays to look at the back of the stamp as well as the front—you never know what you may find!

These illustrations can only hint at the wealth of pleasure and variety to be found in collecting stamps; they have been chosen simply to illustrate a few of the many worthwhile investments, some of the mysteries, and some of the pitfalls which face the beginner. To know and love stamps, you must handle them, study them, and learn from them.

POPULARITY

AND

CONFIDENCE

EVERY COUNTRY in the world is, has been, or will be popular with collectors in one of the major markets. Because of the international nature of the stamp market, interest spreads from one country to another. The investor's problem is to pick the right country for investment, depending on whether he seeks short-term, or long-term appreciation, and to recognize the ones which have already been milked.

In the early days of collecting, philatelists took everything that came along: there were so few stamps that they could attempt an all-world collection without qualms, and their main problem was just in locating the items they needed.

As we have seen, in the United States there has always been a strong market for domestic issues. This was so much so in the early days that several ingenious gentlemen spent their time producing completely bogus "local issues" of non-existent city posts, which they then proceeded to sell to uninformed collectors. The pages of philatelic journals of those days abound in advertisements of bogus material and in heated and libelous denunciations of its producers. South and Central America were also of great interest to U.S. collectors, and this brought about the infamous "Seebeck" contract, which flooded the world market with worthless reprints.

87

British collectors and those in the rest of the English-speaking world have always followed Empire issues closely, and their listing in Volume I of Scott's catalogue gives witness to their popularity in the United States as well. The issues were carefully controlled; because there were few frauds or manipulations of the stamps, consequently they offer a better investment potential as well as, from the purely philatelic viewpoint, a "cleaner" field of collecting. Oddly enough, British stamps have had a far smaller following at home than abroad, and this situation has only changed in recent years with the introduction of more colorful commemorative issues at more frequent intervals, and with the interest aroused by the experimental issues for the graphite and phosphor letter-facing machines.

During World War I, interest turned to "plucky Belgium," France, and the interminable War Tax issues. The postwar years brought many collectors to the field of "Neuropean" stamps, while the inflation issues of a Germany whose economy was falling apart at the seams provided a nine days' wonder.

In the thirties airmail stamps came into their own. Britain had no special airpost stamps, despite continual appeals in the philatelic press at the time, and interest therefore turned to first-flight covers. When the General Post Office organized the first regular internal airmail service without additional air fee, in August 1934, a collection of the first-flight covers ran to over a hundred items, all identical save for the postmarks!

In the United States, airpost stamps came on the scene in 1918, and the very first issue offered collectors one of the world's rarities: the 24¢ value with the Curtiss "Jenny" aircraft in the center inverted. On the day of issue W. T. Roby, a collector, bought one full sheet over the post-office counter. He took the sheet to a dealer who offered him $500 for it, but luckily for him he refused the offer and eventually Eugene Klein, acting on behalf of a syndicate, paid him

$15,000 for it. Then Major Green, a leading collector, purchased the entire sheet for $20,000 and split it up, selling single stamps at $250 each. Copies are now catalogued by Scott's at $25,000 each—for a 24¢ stamp!

Subsequent U.S. airpost issues included the 1930 Graf Zeppelin set. Appearing in the depths of the Depression when few people had money to spare for stamps, the high face value of the set ($4.55 for three stamps) discouraged speculation in what under other conditions would have been a popular issue all over the world. A glance at the catalogue will show how this lack of investment raised the value of the set during the subsequent forty years—a 150-fold increase! And that is just for the straight set: plate-number blocks and first-day covers show far higher rises.

In recent years there have been so many stamps issued that no one pursues more than a few major countries; even to keep up with all the stamps of the British Commonwealth is impossible, and "working back" is out of the question.

At this point collectors began to diversify more than they had done before, taking a specialist interest in minor countries as "sidelines," restricting themselves to fewer countries instead of clamoring to fill all their spaces for a large area. The growth of topical collecting, even in its primitive form of simply collecting the pictures without trying to tell a story with them, was leading to a demand for cleaner material—cancelled-to-order items with their light, unobtrusive postmarks and more mint stamps—and to greater interest in issues of hitherto unpopular countries. All this acted as a spur to postal administrations to produce more, brighter, and better designed stamps, in larger quantities and with more low values for the junior packet trade.

Meanwhile overseas, postwar economic growth in the European nations brought a vastly increased demand for their own stamps, pushing up the prices of the scarcer German and other issues of the immediate postwar period to almost unbelievable heights. Most American dealers were

slow to acknowledge this booming new market, and when
catalogue prices finally came to reflect the international
market there were not sufficient stocks to back them up—they
had all gone back to Europe.

With the break-up of the old links of Empire and the
growing number of British colonies becoming independent,
Commonwealth collecting underwent drastic changes. Newly
independent states tend to issue too many, too gaudy, and
too highly priced stamps in an excess of nationalist enthusiasm and a desire to make some quick money for their
treasuries. Many of them fell willingly into the hands of
private agencies which encouraged these bad habits in
their own interests. The average collector will stand such
goings-on for a short time, but then tends to use "independence" as an excuse to close down on that country's issues
completely. There is no logic about such decisions, any more
than there is in any other collecting choice, and the canny
collector often makes one or two exceptions to the rule if
he is particularly attracted to a country, with all its faults,
and suspects that it will make a good investment.

Japan's rise to economic affluence in the sixties brought
increased home demand for its issues, and these began to
climb up slowly but surely in the world's catalogues until
some of these attractive and well-produced issues became as
popular as the better postwar German issues, and for the
same reason. The early stamps of Japan started a period of
specialist revival, and many catalogue listings were re-
written to take cognizance of rare and previously unaccepted
varieties.

At the same time the Australian and New Zealand markets came into greater prominence, and a rapid spiral in
Pacific Islands prices followed. Not all island groups were
affected at once, and at time of writing there are still neglected areas here which would repay the investor's atten-
tions. Small quantities and limited postal use make these
stamps of real market interest, but, of course, price rises

depend almost entirely on demand, that is, on the fickle popularity with collectors.

Most recent issues of the Communist bloc, issued cancelled-to-order in the millions by propaganda-minded and currency-seeking postal administrations, are not to be regarded on the whole as good investments; however, there is a growing demand for fine-mint copies of some of the better issues, which should be borne in mind by the investor. The major importance of these issues is in their appeal to the junior collector, who can fill his albums with multitudes of colorful labels at little cost. The junior of today is the specialist collector and investor of tomorrow, provided he is not too cruelly wounded when he comes to realize the worthlessness of his gaudy accumulations, and to this extent the Communist issues provide philately with a much-needed boost for years to come. Though we disapprove of the means, we cannot but be grateful for the end product.

This necessarily brief survey points to many of the reasons for popularity: patriotism, economic and political changes in the issuing country, attractive designs, the philatelic policy of a country's postal administration, the availability of material, overseas effects on the U.S. market, the growth in topical collecting, and developments in the collector's own country.

Each of these points is important, and each should be considered whenever one evaluates the possibilities of a country or even of a particular issue. We have seen that even unpopular countries can produce worthwhile investment material if the subject of the issue is popular; by the same token, a popular country can kill its own market by producing unacceptable items.

The size of the market inside the country itself is always of importance. In advanced countries like the United States, Britain, and those of Western Europe there have always been large numbers of patriotic collectors who support their home product first. When Germany was a colonial power Germans collected the stamps of its colonies, but once control passed to other countries these early issues went into a decline, from which in some cases they have yet to recover.

Germany provides a textbook example of the effect that internal economic developments have on the market for a country's own issues. In the Nazi period contemporary issues were avidly collected, as were the special Nazi postmarks and other symbols of the state. With the collapse of the Reich the German people feared that possession of these items might bring retribution from the Allied occupiers (this actually happened in East Germany), and many, faced with dire poverty, were forced to sell their stamps for a fraction of their value merely to live. The contemporary issues were little collected, since there was no money to spare, and the stamp-issuing policies of the various constituent bodies into which the country had been split were contradictory, confusing, and changeable. One result of this is that the "Towns" issues of 1945, though extremely scarce and with a high catalogue price, are still far less popular than they should be.

Economic regrowth in West Germany brought a renewed demand for stamps. Stamp clubs opened in schools and workmen's clubs, and the new issues were eagerly snapped up in full sheets. This brought the realization that stocks of the stamps of the 1949–54 period were not to be found, especially in mint condition, and these were the first to rocket upward. The Germans had not been able to afford them at date of issue, and nobody else seemed to want the early issues of this republic formed out of a defeated and truncated totalitarian state!

The rapid improvement of these stamps brought increased investment in more recent issues, while gradually collectors started to work backward to the Nazi period and the Weimar Republic and then to the earliest issues of the old German Empire and the Old German States stamps.

Increased investment started to affect all these, and it seemed as though the German market would continue to improve forever. Of course, there had to be a break, and this came when many of the small investors who had stockpiled the by-no-means-scarce later issues tried to realize some of their paper profits. The flood of this material onto the open market could not be absorbed, some panic selling took place and brought prices even lower, and only the real investment items—the scarcer postwar issues and the classic "blue chip" items—managed to hold up as all fell around them.

So we see that lack of confidence can have a devastating effect on stamp investment, as it does in transactions on the stock exchange or in any business where value is based on popularity and not on commodity use. When the German investors came to disbelieve in the worth of their stockpiled sheets as investment currency, so their value dropped. The fluctuations in the Italian market, previously referred to, are another example of this, and it is noteworthy that along with the German slump came a similar recession in the over-bought issues of Switzerland and Liechtenstein and to a lesser extent Austria, where a similar investment pattern had existed and where confidence was subtly undermined by news of the German slump.

Israel provides an example of how economic conditions can affect the stamp market. With Jews living throughout the world, Israeli stamps are, of course, assured of a basic overseas market, yet prices have fluctuated wildly since the state was proclaimed in 1948.

As is usual with new states, early issues were under-bought, and the interesting tabs along the bottom of the sheet were generally ignored by both collectors and dealers for some years. By far the greater proportion were sold as single stamps with the tabs torn off and thrown away, and many collectors even detached the tabs and destroyed them before mounting the stamps. Israeli tabs were designed to tell more about the stamps themselves; they form the lower sheet margin of every issue except the postage-dues, and after a while they became so popular that in 1957 special printings were made for collectors with tabs on every stamp.

As Israel showed its strength in the face of Arab aggression there came a growth in collector interest, and by the mid-fifties all prices, especially those for the scarce early issues with tabs, had grown immensely. However, the country's economy was far from firm, and a sudden crisis of confidence brought the whole edifice tumbling down. Lucky —or canny—collectors made fine profits by selling out at the right moment, while those who bought at the height of the boom suffered badly when they came to unload during the slump.

Israel's clean philatelic policy, the attractive designs of its stamps, and the free availability of large stocks brought a slow rise in interest, but prices never really recovered until the Six Day War, when massively renewed popularity showed itself in rapid rises on the U.S. market and American dealers started to take full-page buying advertisements in British collectors' journals in the hopes of replenishing their stocks. Israel represents an unknown quantity as to long-term philatelic investment, but it is a country which will always bear close watching and the earlier issues are without doubt "blue chips." A warning to neophytes: Beware of forgeries, faked postmarks and regummed "mint" stamps!

The attractiveness of a country's stamps has a strong bearing on their appeal to collectors. It was the growth in interest in Britain's attractive commemorative and special sets which gradually brought collectors to take up the phosphor-lined varieties, then the more recent regular stamps, and slowly the market rise spread further back. This is a frequent occurrence in philatelic investment, and should never be forgotten by the investor. Whenever collectors start to clamor for new issues of a country, the wise investor will immediately seek out the earlier sets, before the rise spreads backward. It won't always work, of course—nothing is completely predictable, but this is one of the surest trends in philately.

In the same way, one can assume that an interest in postal history will follow a rise in stamp prices for almost any country. The canny collector was the one who, when Pitcairn Island's stamps started to rise, scouted around and picked up examples of New Zealand and British stamps used on covers from Pitcairn, ship covers and markings, and anything even remotely connected with the field, before the average collector had even begun to realize that they existed.

Between 1808 and 1856 (when the Pitcairn Islanders were evacuated to Norfolk Island) many ships visited the island, yet only one cover appears to have survived from this time. Its scarcity may not have been recognized when it was auctioned in 1966, as this was prior to the boom in Pitcairn material, and it realized only $133. Were it to appear on the market again, this price would now be greatly surpassed—$500 would sound reasonable.

We have seen that where there is a large international demand for a country's issues, as with the Vatican and Israel, the size of the home market is unimportant. This also applies to the stamps of the United Nations which, thanks to the sane philatelic policy of the postal administration and to its good publicity, have always been popular with collectors all over the world. The stamps are valid for use only from the U.N. Headquarters in New York and Geneva, but command a wide following by virtue of the organization's importance in the world.

Yet even here one finds that the New York issues are most popular with American collectors; the separate issues of the U.N. agencies in Geneva are more collected in Switzerland, as are those of the old League of Nations, so even in this avowedly international sphere patriotic sentiments are reflected in collecting habits.

Strictly philatelic considerations can affect popularity, as was seen in the takeover by Mardons of Salisbury of all the printing of Rhodesian stamps when Rhodesia declared its independence. The Mardon printings have tremendous interest from a purely philatelic viewpoint, and their study has presented modern collectors with a fine opportunity to follow the development of printing and gumming techniques in a limited field. Only the British Government's restrictions on the importation and possession of these stamps has brought the study to a halt in Britain and, to a lesser extent, in other countries honoring the United Nations embargo on exports from Rhodesia, and there is no doubt that when the regulations are abolished there will be a great upsurge of interest in these issues, perhaps restoring Rhodesian philately to the peak of popularity which it enjoyed in the twenties.

ADVERSE

SIGNS

WE HAVE SEEN how loss of confidence in a country's investment potential can bring a slump. Apart from considerations of patriotism, fears for the economic stability of the issuing country, and overinvestment, changes in the philatelic policy of the postal administration can bring dissatisfaction and loss of interest almost overnight.

During the last century, several South American nations signed an agreement with a speculator whereby he would supply all their stamps for postal use free of charge, on the understanding that issues would be withdrawn and invalidated regularly and that he would have the right to produce unlimited reprints from the original plates after withdrawal from postal use.

Soon the market was flooded with these "Seebecks," and philatelists realized that it was pointless to purchase current stamps at face value from these countries, since the reprints were indistinguishable and would be available in years to come at a fraction of the face value. The popularity of these countries dwindled and has yet to be restored.

In addition to their immense cancelling-to-order operations, certain Communist nations reuse old printing plates to produce further quantities of the stamps after their withdrawal from postal use. In certain Communist Chinese issues the reprints *are* distinguishable, but this does not apply to all.

97

It is difficult to see how investment potential can exist in the issues of any country where the official stamp-export organization is able to produce more stocks whenever required.

In recent years many small countries have handed over their stamp production and distribution to private agencies. There is nothing intrinsically wrong with this practice, so long as strict control is exercised over the activities of the commercial organization, which is, naturally, interested solely in producing as high an income as possible in the shortest possible time. However, such control is often not exercised, and many countries with formerly reasonable stamp-issuing policies have suddenly given birth to multiple issues of high face value, with limited or nonexistent postal use, and with topics having little or no connection with the country. Miniature sheets, color changes, imperforate limited releases, se-tenant blocks, and other philatelic frivolities have appeared, and have been pressure-sold to unsuspecting collectors by wide-scale publicity campaigns. Overproduction has led to cancellation-to-order of remainders, in order to dispose of surplus stocks at cut prices, and to other unethical practices.

There are many such examples; Paraguay and Panama are paramount offenders. Many recent issues of these and other countries are not listed in Scott's catalogue; they are instead relegated to a separate booklet, *For the Record*, to indicate their dubious philatelic status.

The production of obviously planned "errors" in limited quantities has been the cause of many countries losing their popularity, especially where the varieties are created through local overprinting. In some cases these spurious issues are available to the collector and dealer only through the agency, or one of its associate firms, at enhanced prices. There are usually many protestations of innocence from the agency and the postal administration, but after a while these begin to ring hollow to the sensible collector. The investor, of course, will have learned to give the country a wide berth long before things reach this stage.

The new-issue dealer, ordering from an agency or directly from the issuing country, realizes an occasional windfall in his unrewarding task: the acquisition at face value of stamps showing a major error. Where such errors occur in some profusion but somehow fail to turn up in the stocks of new-issue dealers, the trade naturally becomes suspicious. Libel laws make it difficult for outright denunciations to be made, but you may rest assured that the word soon gets around the trade and hints of knavery can be found "between the lines" of published comment.

Another agency gimmick is "crank" items, such as free-form or coin-shaped labels, self-adhesive stickers, or miniature sheets printed on nylon (which, in one case, could not be stuck to a cover and from which the postmark could be easily washed off!). Unnecessary overprints produced at short notice and in grossly inadequate quantities are another warning sign—although we have seen that in cases of national upheaval or disaster such short-lived provisional sets are acceptable.

However, there is no denying that in the case of a country with a clean philatelic past which goes over to agency manipulations for a short time and then reverts to proper stamp-issuing policy, the discredited issues in time come to acquire first a curiosity interest and then a spurious respectability. And when the scandals of the past no longer arouse outraged indignation these items are sought after by serious collectors intent on "completeness." Much as one may deprecate the impact of the agencies on stamp-issuing policies, it is true that in time much is forgotten and forgiven— a fact that should not be overlooked by the investor with *long-term* profit in mind.

One example of a country which has suffered a number of philatelic scandals, and which is currently in the hands of a "dynamic" agency producing metal-foil coin-shaped items, imperforate overprints in changed colors, and so forth, is Tonga. Toward the end of the last century the postmaster of Tonga came to a private arrangement whereby large quantities of stamps were printed, passed directly to him without being officially accounted for, then cancelled-to-order and sold direct to dealers at a large discount off the face value. On one occasion alone, 105,000 stamps were sold to a German dealer for $1,000, and all these came on the philatelic market.

Yet a glance at the catalogue will show that these stamps, where cancelled-to-order sets cannot easily be distinguished from some of the genuinely postmarked ones, command a high price. Here, however, a word to the investor is in order: the overprinted and surcharged issues of Tonga around this time were not, so far as is known, speculated in this way, and should therefore be a far better bet at current prices.

Both overproduction and uninformed investment can bring about bad market conditions, and a prime example of this lies in the stamps of the United States. Here there is a constant turnover of new collectors, many of whom patriotically put aside full sheets of all the low-value commemorative issues, which are printed in quantities of many millions. Of all these stamps only the plate-blocks of certain issues have any scarcity value at all, so after a while each generation of disillusioned collectors begins to dispose of its sheets and blocks at well under face value, swearing never to be caught by stamp collecting again. The discounted stamps are bought up in quantity by brokers who sell them, still below face value, to business houses with large mailing lists. And so a major function of the average U.S. collector is to provide cheap postage for these firms!

More wealthy American collectors have tended to be attracted, again in an insular way, to the "limited issues" of certain South American nations and to the stamps of countries where there is heavy American investment in other fields, such as Laos and the Ryukyu Islands, a chain in the

Pacific south of Japan under U.S. administration since World War II. We have already mentioned Paraguay, and while the stamps of Laos are attractive and produced in essentially small quantities (they are also popular in France), the American collector tends to take up such items as presentation sheets and imperforate varieties, which have little philatelic importance but which by virtue of their scarcity come to demand extremely high prices.

So long as the demand for these monstrosities exists there will be agencies which will produce them, but an economic recession in America or a change of heart by American investors could well bring them down to the level of non-postal labels, which in the main they are.

In conclusion, one may say that on the whole a small, philatelically clean country, with a genuine postal need for its stamps and with small but carefully controlled printings, will provide the most satisfactory long-term investment. The other major category of investment material comes from countries which have a large and growing collector demand inside the country itself—but here the investor is warned: this can lead to stockpiling of recent issues, which, if dumped on the open market in too large quantities, will deflate the whole market.

UNTOUCHED

AREAS

THE WISE INVESTOR will hedge his bets by taking up one or
more currently unpopular countries or topics, so long as they
are "clean" and the stamps have a justifiable existence.

He should set out to complete *all* the stamp issues of his
chosen country, and will no doubt discover that (1) dealers
do not want his business; (2) foreign sources of material
may be more reliable but will almost certainly quote prices
in excess of those shown in Scott's catalogue; (3) there are
certain stamps—often odd values in otherwise easily purchased sets—which are far more elusive than the catalogue
would lead him to expect. This is the point at which cash
ceases to matter: these are the stamps he *must* have, as they
are obviously the "blue chips" of the future.

Nepal is certainly not a popular country. Its early stamps
are primitive, abounding in varieties and flaws, and are
hard to come by. Yet the earlier issues *can* be completed
with time and care, except for one or two *tête-bêche* (reversed in relation to each other) pairs of immense scarcity.
Later commemoratives, though elusive, are not impossible
to obtain piecemeal, and soon the collector will feel that
he is well on the way to completion. Until he comes to recognize—and be continually irritated by—the one space left
by his lack of a 1-rupee stamp issued in 1956 and catalogued in Scott's at a ludicrously low figure both mint and

used. Further investigation reveals that only *two thousand* copies of this stamp were printed! Needless to say, it is far more important to acquire a copy of this stamp than to build up a specialized selection of the early stamps.

Few collectors seem to appreciate the philosophy behind this. They become attracted to a country's stamps, and their first aim is to acquire as many of the stamps as they can. Only then do they think of filling the gaps where individual stamps are highly catalogued, and they may well resign themselves to having permanent gaps here. This is all right so long as the aim is pleasure, but where profit is concerned it is of prime importance to make sure of all the "good" stamps first of all, regardless of cost or difficulty. This is where an investment sideline can pay immediate dividends, since its liquidation as a lot will provide the collector with the cash needed to make an impressive showing in his specialty. In fact, it may well be worth his while to sell off some other unconsidered items at a loss in order to raise the cash.

Having started on the path to philatelic completion, the investor should also take a look at the postal history of his chosen field and set out to acquire at least some of the plums in the pre-stamp and postmark areas. The acquisition of cheaper items again can be left until later, although it makes sense to get all the current material direct from the issuing country at once, in case any should suddenly become obsolete without warning.

This probably sounds like a lot of hard work, but consider this: if the collector sets out in the ordinary way, he treads the same path, only more slowly. But while he takes his time, others get in ahead of him: demand increases, prices rise, and he is farther than ever from his goal.

Of course, all this applies to fields where some records exist, where a society or a single collector has done sufficient spade work so that the newcomer can just pick up the information and be on his way. The really interesting thing to do is to try, if only as a part-time sideline, to find another area of collecting where the spade work has never been properly done, and do it yourself.

But before examining the exotic byways of philately, let us make a brief survey of some of the countries which have been neglected and which offer a reasonable opening for the investor who is prepared to take some trouble in searching out material. None of these can really be called an "untouched area," since each has at least a small following, but all of them are likely in years to come to have a fair chance of hitting the big time. And even if they never climb to dizzy heights, they offer the collector a chance to build up a personal collection in a field with little competition.

AROUND

THE WORLD

MANY YEARS AGO Scott's catalogue was split into two parts. There are so many stamps and so many countries that an all-world listing is just too cumbersome.

The simplest way to divide the world, it was decided, was to list all the most popular countries in one volume and lump the rest together in a second. Volume 1 starts off with the United States and its possessions, then the United Nations, continues with Great Britain and the entire British Commonwealth, and passes on to the nations of Central and South America. Volume 2 covers European countries and their colonies, and the rest of the world.

It sounds a straightforward arrangement—but don't imagine that it is a logical one! I doubt if there *is* a logical way of splitting the countries of the world into two, three, or even four roughly equal parts. Scott's arrangement is for convenience, is quite arbitrary, and unfortunately has the effect of distorting the collector's view of the world.

Here are a few examples of the oddities that occur: although all the Canal Zone issues were in fact produced under U.S. administration, as were all those in the short stamp existence of Guam, and although Puerto Rico and the Philippines have also used stamps of Spain and since independence the Philippines have had their own stamps, all of these issues are relegated to Volume 2. Fair enough,

you say—they are not U.S. stamps. But the listings for the
Danish West Indies (now the U.S. Virgin Islands) comprise nothing but foreign stamps, as do most of the Hawaiian
lists, and these are in Volume 1. The reason given for this
discrepancy is "philatelic custom." Yet *all* the stamps of
Cuba—Spanish and independent as well as U.S. issues—
are listed together, not under "U.S. Possessions" but with the
rest of Latin America. Immediately following "U.S. Possessions" are the New York issues of the United Nations, while
some of the Geneva stamps of the same organization are
placed in Volume 2. Yet it is the same body!

Further strange things are found when we come to the
British Commonwealth section, which contains lists of Egypt,
Iraq, Jordan, and Nepal (all omitted from Commonwealth
catalogues by British publishers) as well as Burma, Ireland,
Orange Free State, South Africa, and many others for which
there is equally no political excuse but which oddly enough
are in British-published Commonwealth catalogues. The reason stated for these anomalies is that they are "included for
the convenience of collectors."

All this is said in no spirit of criticism of the catalogue
editors. They have to please the majority of collectors, and
philatelists are notoriously conservative. When the division
into two parts took place, there was good reason for most
of these decisions.

The real point for the collector to remember is that he
need not be bound by any of these conventions. If he
chooses to treat Cuba as though the U.S. issues form a
single collectable group, he may do so—and he will find
plenty of interest and value in them. If he chooses to stop
all his Commonwealth collections as each country obtains
independence, he will certainly not be alone. And if he decides to arrange the U.S. issues of the Philippines after the
Spanish ones and before the independent issues, he has many
good arguments for doing so, particularly when dealing with
postal-history aspects.

When he comes to consider the investment potential of his collection, he must remember that, all other things being equal, a country in Volume 1 will be in greater demand than one in Volume 2, and this fact will affect prices, investment potential, and the cost of his stamps from dealers—not to mention the availability of out-of-the-way material. It is true that more people spend more money on the Volume 1 listings, but it does not follow that the sensible investor will always do the same. The following survey of countries will give a few pointers on these problems.

VOLUME 1

This opens with the postal issues of the United States, in considerable detail. Even more specialized lists are found in Scott's United States Specialized Stamp Catalogue, and any collector interested in doing more than just filling gaps in an album should certainly possess this book. It also contains non-postal items, but here caution is recommended: while these may hold considerable interest, their attraction for the investor is likely to be much less.

The main point to remember about U.S. stamps is that in the past forty years, with few exceptions, they have been overbought. The exceptions are unlikely to hold much scope either, as their potential is already well known; they are nonetheless "blue chip" material, almost guaranteed to move up slowly but surely forever.

Much more scope exists in taking a single early issue—preferably one which is still cheap and plentiful—and examining it in real depth from both a philatelic and a postal-history viewpoint. The late Harry F. Allen built up a world-famous collection based on a single stamp, the "Black Jack," which filled six volumes, covering the domestic and overseas uses of the stamp, its cancellations, the Civil War period. Such was the scope of the collection and the philatelic importance of its findings that it inspired a $10 book published by the American Philatelic Society.

A problem with U.S. philately is that little material exists overseas. It has all been bought up and brought home, and so the impetus given to the market in other countries' issues by the international flow of material is almost lacking in this case. Far too many American collectors show only a cursory interest in foreign stamps, and as a result there is a sameness about dealers' stocks (which are built up to sell well, of course), and thus a self-perpetuating narrowness in American philately. A side effect of this isolationism is that when they do venture outside the confines of all-American stampdom, many collectors fall prey to the depredations of the cancelled-to-order and limited-issue merchants. One of the aims of this book is to encourage a greater diversification among stateside collectors, which will be to their own benefit and to the good of the hobby as a whole.

Scott's specialized listings give catalogue prices for such items as plate numbers; although these may well serve to fix dealers' prices, in most cases the collector will find considerable difficulty in disposing of his own stamps at anything approaching these figures. This is not a plot on the part of the trade, but merely a reflection of the overabundance of this type of material available, and this situation is unlikely to change.

Aside from the straightforward listings, the U.S. section includes such enticements to the wealthy collector as the Carriers stamps and those of the Confederate states. Although these are not fields for the newcomer to tread, they fall into the "blue chip" category and cannot but be recommended to the advanced philatelist of more than ordinary means. The territory is well worked over already, but this country is big enough to conceal undiscovered treasures even more than a century later.

Of the U.S. possessions, there is no doubt that Hawaii offers the best investment, especially in view of recent interest in the Pacific as a whole. But again a deep pocket is needed, and the newer collector is recommended to look elsewhere for less well worked-over material. Stamps of the United Nations in New York are perennially popular but they too suffer from overinvestment, and there is little scope here for "sideline" collections off the beaten path.

With Great Britain we come to the most popular overseas country, and one which like the United States offers more than enough to keep a thousand collectors occupied for a lifetime. The strength of the British market is such that there can never be a lasting slump in these stamps, and even the overbought commemoratives of the 1964–70 period, which in 1970 suffered a heavy blow from dumping, will come into their own again. What happened here is that too many uninformed investors started stockpiling massive quantities of new issues as they appeared, in the mistaken belief that because the comparatively scarce commemoratives of 1953–61 had risen drastically the same was predestined for their own acquisitions.

Once the investors tired of holding their stocks—and this didn't take long—they found that the spiral in prices had been brought about not by collector demand but by their own manipulation of the market. Nobody else wanted full sheets of recent issues, and they were forced to unload them at below face value because, with the coming of the decimal monetary system, there would no longer be even a *postal* use for their stamps. Knowing the brokerage terms for modern mint U.S. issues, one can perhaps imagine what would happen to the domestic market if the government announced that in a year's time all previous issues were to be demonetized. This was the position in Britain in 1970, and had it not been for the international interest aroused by London's exhibition in that year things might have been worse.

As it was, that interest addressed itself mainly to early "classic" issues of Britain, with a consequent hardening in prices for fine material of the nineteenth century and renewed rises for Edwardian and earlier Georgian stamps. There is still plenty of scope for careful buying in the 1840–70 era, and even today, after more than a century of determined study, postal history offers some real bargains.

The British Commonwealth presents a very patchy picture, ranging from worked-out countries through currently booming material to untouched sleepers. Of considerable interest are stamps of Britain overprinted for use in Morocco and also during World War II in North Africa. Morocco Agencies issues are complex and have already been well explored, but the other overprints are currently less popular and may provide some surprises in future.

Aden, next in the book, is a dead duck now but may still have some scope for long-term investment. The collector is warned off most of the subsequent issues of South Arabia and the Aden States; with these can be classed the stamps of Ajman, Sharjah, and other Arab sheikdoms in the area.

Anguilla rates only a footnote mention in Scott's catalogue for the stamps issued after its declaration of independence in 1967. This is a pity, as the stamps have a genuine popularity and are well regarded in Britain and elsewhere.

With Antigua the catalogue starts off the large and complex group of West Indian islands deservedly popular with collectors throughout the world. The scope is enormous but in many cases already well worked over; the interested collector is recommended to look for a small area and study it intensively rather than attack the whole group and fail.

With Ascension we come to a group categorized as "small islands." St. Helena and Tristan da Cunha are others, and it is axiomatic that if a small island has not already hit the jackpot, it will, provided its policy is clean. All three mentioned are sought after and are unlikely to suffer anything more than a temporary slump at any time.

Australia offers a tremendous field for the specialist and is already well on the way up. The pure investor might buy every high-value Kangaroo stamp he is offered at a percentage off catalogue, then just sit tight. The more humble collector is warned that he is in for a long and bitter struggle unless—an excellent idea—he starts with the decimal issues and builds up a really specialized collection from that date; there are already some real scarcities in this field, and more will follow.

The Australian states have all been worked over again and again, with consequent high catalogue prices. Six states issued stamps prior to the introduction of a unified Commonwealth issue, and at this point we come to an extremely important discovery—one which will be referred to again in connection with other countries, and which no collector should ignore.

It concerns catalogues: although Scott's is the most popular in the United States, with Minkus running second, there are other listings prepared abroad which for certain purposes are essential reading. For a start, it is axiomatic that the stamps of any large and literate country will be more collected and more studied at home than abroad; consequently, more detailed catalogues will be prepared there and these will contain information unknown to most American collectors. Many valuable varieties of stamps, differing only slightly from the standard type, can be found in dealers' stocks at very low prices because, being unlisted in Scott's catalogue, they are just not recognized for what they are. Needless to say, the acquisition of such items can pay very great dividends, in the same way that a European collector using Scott's can pick up rare U.S. material in his own country because its nature is not appreciated by the seller.

Nowadays dealers are becoming more and more aware of this factor, and particularly in Britain—where so much of the stamp trade is concerned with export business—it is not unusual to find a dealer selling U.S. issues by Scott's numbers; European stamps by the Yvert, Zumstein, or Michel catalogue according to country; Israel by Mosden's or

Simon's catalogue; and using specialized one-country lists to identify and price issues of many smaller countries from the Netherlands to Japan.

In checking Scott's Australian States listings against those of Stanley Gibbons' British Commonwealth catalogue, one finds that in every case Gibbons' list is at least twice as long! Where Scott's list shows a single stamp valued at, let us say, $50, Gibbons may indicate the existence of three shades, valued at $20, $50, and $175. Obviously the first is overpriced by Scott's and the third, if bought by that list, is a bargain: it pays to know these things.

Almost without exception, Gibbons' catalogue gives more information on British Commonwealth issues, particularly on older stamps. For stamps of Queen Elizabeth's reign there is an even more detailed catalogue available, the *Elizabethan,* which gives details of quantities issued, withdrawal dates, and a multitude of other valuable facts. For Great Britain itself there is a really specialized handbook in three volumes, also published by Gibbons, a *sine qua non* for the specialist.

Reverting to the Australian states, the important point to remember is that they have a small but perennial popularity in Australia itself and a fair following in Britain, and that consequently prices are rather on the high side. One must be particularly careful about the condition of stamps offered for sale, and there are also forgeries to contend with. If you are really keen to take up one of these complex countries, I would recommend Western Australia as the one offering the best chance of improvement in years to come.

The B.C.O.F. overprints on Australian stamps, for use in Japan just after the war, are an example of the dictum that it pays to pick up unconsidered trifles before they catch the public eye: it's a bit late now. The Australian Antarctic Territory brings us to another internationally popular field, polar philately. Australian stamps were in use first in this area, and covers bearing these with Antarctic postmarks carry a very high premium.

Also in the Antarctic field are the Ross Dependency of New Zealand, the British Antarctic Territory (part of what used to be known as the Falkland Islands Dependencies) and South Georgia and the Falklands issues themselves. There is a certain amount of skepticism attached to these— how many islands with a population of penguins plus a few scientists really need stamps? In the case of the Falklands, a shadow is cast over the group by the possibility that the islands may be handed over to Argentina, which claims them and which has issued several stamps depicting them as Argentinian property. However, the newer territories offer the opportunity of starting at "number one" quite cheaply, always an attraction to the beginning collector.

There are, of course, Antarctic topicals from other countries, and covers from the U.S. Task Forces in the area have a strong following. If the idea of an all-Antarctic collection appeals to you, bear in mind that it is likely to be a long and expensive task to approach completion—but I consider it to be one of the top investment fields in the world.

The Bahamas, Barbados, and Barbuda come into the general West Indies heading already discussed; perhaps a warning is due about the many modern issues of Barbuda, which are produced by an aggressive agency and well publicized. There is not likely to be any potential in these stamps for a considerable time: it is doubtful whether they really serve any postal function, and they seem to be appearing too quickly for the average collector to stomach. These issues are not listed by Scott's except in the *For the Record* supplement, but at least one extended series, depicting all the monarchs of England, is likely to have a considerable following. Maximum cards and first-day covers (which I shall refer to later) of this small topical issue might profitably be pursued, despite the cataloguer's stand.

Africa is not currently a popular continent with investors, although there are some exceptions. Basutoland (now Lesotho), Bechuanaland (now Botswana), and Swaziland offer decimal surcharges of some complexity and expense, as well as interesting and increasingly valuable other issues. Malawi (formerly Nyasaland) and the various Rhodesian issues form another group, which can be extended to cover German Africa and occupation issues; this is a comprehensive and expensive area to do properly, and one might instead split off a smaller section for detailed study. Kenya, Uganda, and Tanganyika (now Tanzania) also have German forerunners, complex changes of title and issues, and a mixed political background which will deter many but may still offer tremendous interest. Nigeria is another area with a checkered past, and listed with it are the short-lived Biafran issues; these last stamps I would recommend only if used on covers.

South Africa has always had a strong following, and includes the Cape of Good Hope, Natal, Boer War material, South-West Africa issues, and a wealth of specialist items. This is another big group to tackle, but it has its adherents and shows slow but steady appreciation with some real blue chips and, I feel, many sleepers. However, the new collector is warned about reprints of Transvaal issues and forgeries in the postal-history field.

Brunei falls into the Malayan group, and here there is a profusion of issues to attract the collector: the 13 different series for the Malay States, those of Labuan, Sarawak, North Borneo (Sabah), Singapore, the British Military Administration, and the Japanese-occupation issues, which are both expensive and widely forged. Brunei can, however, be taken by itself; it offers considerable interest and the chance of being a late-starting "pop" country (I hope I am not too late with this tip!). Any of the other territories can also be taken in isolation, but what this gains in simplification it loses from the postal-history viewpoint.

The Maldives, in the Indian Ocean, offer interesting

postal history but an interminable sequence of gaudy and unrecommendable agency issues. Mauritius and the Seychelles, on the other hand, are blue-chip countries and out of the reach of the smaller collector—but highly recommended to the wealthy investor. As a consolation prize, this area offers the new British Indian Ocean Territory, where starting from "number one" is easy—make sure of postmarks and the rest as well, and don't miss a thing.

Ceylon, Burma, and India are all countries which have had their day; it may come again, and all early issues are good investment material provided condition is fine, but it is hard to see the multitudes of modern Indian low-value commemoratives as ever being any better than packet material. Certainly one can only look on them as "long shots" for investment, especially the post-independence issues. Pakistan offers the fascinating local overprints which heralded the new state, and many errors on the "paisa" new-currency overprints, but these are unpopular and suspected of faking. The collector is warned off the stamps of Bahawalpur available at fantastic discounts off catalogue price.

Taking in a few oddments: listings for Palestine are far from complete, and the country offers more to the specialist than one would imagine; as forerunners of Israeli stamps they are particularly popular. Hong Kong has a long and honorable philatelic history and ranks in the blue-chip brigade. British Guiana (now Guyana) offers the world's rarest stamp (the 1¢ black-on-magenta of 1856), other valuable items, and a slow falling-off in interest and popularity from that point on; it is well thought of in the United States and therefore cannot be recommended to the more humble collector! British Honduras—just a big question mark here, because of the political situation at the time of writing this book.

Canada has its constituent parts—New Brunswick, Newfoundland, Nova Scotia, and so forth—scattered through the catalogue. Much blue-chip material is here, most of it al-

ready high-priced, and multitudes of low-value commemoratives, few of which will ever move much. Regular stamps
offer plenty of scope for study with booklet panes, coils, and
early phosphor-tagged issues. All the issues have been well
worked over, as they fall within the purview of the U.S.
market as well as having a permanent attraction to collectors of British colonial stamps.

New Zealand has also always had its followers, but there
are certain areas which have never appreciated properly,
including many of the "Official" overprints, where quantities
are remarkably low. There is immense scope for specialization, and the newcomer is recommended to start with the
post-decimalization issues and do them properly rather than
make an unsuccessful stab at covering everything. For the
investor this is blue-chip country.

The New Zealand Dependencies offer great scope for
investment and collecting, all the issues having a long way
to go. The early Antarctic expedition issues need no further
comment, while the Cook Islands issues cover a vast range
of material from the earliest days up to the present agency
issues; in this Group lie Aitutaki, Niue, and Penrhyn, all of
which should be treated as part of one collection. Samoa
offers an immense field for the conscientious collector and
investor—many of these stamps have stood still for so long
that they can now only move upward: this may happen very
speedily. In all cases, postal-history material is very important; that for Samoa takes in the period of German
control.

The rest of the Pacific offers much to the collector. The
Solomons are philatelically clean, as are the Gilberts; in
both cases don't forget the wartime period when armed-
forces post offices used stamps of many nations. Both are
highly recommended even at this late date, as are the New
Hebrides—and *please* don't imagine that the French issues
are for a different place: both are used together by the same
people at the same offices, and Scott's separate listings of
the stamps in two catalogues are sheer lunacy.

Fiji is one of the most complex studies in the Pacific. Early issues are often very expensive, and there is tremendous scope in the postal history of the group. Modern issues are attractive and offer scope for study, but consider your purse carefully before you rush into the lot. Tonga presents a similar picture, but bedeviled by speculation and scandal and currently functioning under "dynamic" agency control which is, to say the least, off-putting. With Pitcairn we come to a perfect example of what can happen—with a vengeance —to very recent stamps when a small island comes into the public eye.

The last group of Commonwealth countries are those with affinities with Europe: Cyprus, Gibraltar, Ireland, and Malta. All have spiraled upward in recent years with increased European investment; all offer some blue chips and some still unawakened issues; all are now a bit too far on the route for the newcomer to make an easy entry, and the investor is advised to restrict himself to the very best items, and not to hold them too long.

In conclusion, there is one thing the British Commonwealth collector should always be aware of: the group of stamps known generally as "used abroads." Many countries' issues can be found with postmarks of other countries— Australia, New Zealand, India, and, of course, Great Britain are prime examples, but others exist. Whatever the reason (and there are many) for these items' existence, they are all important, and almost all such postmarks will be far more valuable than the basic stamps. It is sheer vandalism and stupidity to soak them off a cover, and you should always be on the *qui vive* for anything like this which the average collector may have overlooked.

The "American Nations" category takes up some four hundred pages in Scott's catalogue. Naturally, they have a devoted following among American collectors, but unfortunately in many cases this has led to unquestioning acceptance of unnecessary issues and varieties.

In recent years Scott's *For the Record* listing has helped

to purge the catalogue of many issues for which little justifi-
cation can be found, but there is still a great deal of dead
wood among the older issues listed. There is no denying,
however, that a great deal of interest can be found in this
part of the world; the problem lies in separating this from the
speculative material.

The general picture, which applies to a greater or lesser
extent to all these countries, is of complicated and well-
researched early issues, some valuable but many merely old,
followed by a large number of short sets or single commemorative stamps, with many changes in regular issues
and a quite disproportionate amount of overprinting. Air
stamps exist in large numbers, reflecting American collector
interest in this field, and there is a plethora of "Official"
stamps, usually overprints again, and special issues for express and other mail.

In deciding which of these countries to take up, the
collector should first consider the sheer quantity of different
stamps and, second, he should evaluate the catalogue values,
watching out particularly for reprinted issues (Seebecks and
so forth) which may be regarded as worthless for investment, and for the other extreme—stamps which are priced
so high that they may be forever out of his reach. Only if
these factors are acceptable should further consideration be
given to pursuing the collection.

Taking the countries in order, we find that Argentina
provides a reasonably cheap subject on the whole, including
many proofs and color trials, many of which may still be
acquired relatively cheaply. There is plenty of variety among
more modern issues, and some of them, particularly the
annual Army Day and Navy Day stamps, have an extremely
high standard of design. The interesting local issues for
Buenos Aires, Cordoba, and Corrientes offer scope for the
advanced collector if his pocketbook is deep enough.

Bolivia's issues follow the same pattern, as do those of
Chile and Colombia; the latter offers many local issues, and

a serious study of these short-lived series can provide both philatelic and political interest as well as, in some cases, a worthwhile investment.

Brazil offers the world's second-oldest stamp issue, following only three years after Britain's Penny Black. An intriguing note follows the 1930 issues in Scott's catalogue, indicating that since that date imperforate or part-perforated sheets of nearly all commemorative issues "seem to have been available to a few collectors or dealers." From the guarded nature of this comment, and the fact that these varieties are not given catalogue status, the collector can draw his own conclusions. The situation is, however, symptomatic of a weakness from which too many postal administrations suffer—the desire to pander to the craze for "rare" oddities—and equally to a failing among collectors themselves to distinguish between *postal* material and that produced purely to appeal to cupidity. In any case, I feel that Brazil produces rather too many stamps, but design standards are improving and this may lead to a rise in collector interest.

Cuba is a fascinating country. Complex Spanish and U.S. administration issues are followed by the popular stamps of the republic under U.S. military rule. There is unlikely to be any real movement among these issues, however, especially while stamps of the Castro regime are banned from importation. If the U.S. Government relents at a later date and these issues are given catalogue status, there is bound to be a vast upsurge in interest which may affect prices for earlier issues as well.

The Dominican Republic follows the usual pattern, but with Ecuador we come to a country which has blotted its philatelic reputation thoroughly and, one would feel, irretrievably. Although there is much of real interest among earlier issues, the air stamps of the thirties bring with them some dubious varieties, and the country's modern policy leads me to put it on my "treat with extreme caution" list, along with Panama, Paraguay, and to a lesser extent Haiti and Nicaragua.

Little can be added about Guatemala, Honduras, Mexico, and Peru, although each has its attractions and its areas of special interest. Peruvian locals are specialist material and not recommended for the novice. Salvador and Uruguay follow the standard pattern, and so we come at last to Venezuela, perhaps one of the more attractive countries, but whose issues are little different in style or in investment potential from the others.

Nobody, I am sure, will ever persuade American collectors to desert these countries, but everyone should remember that there is a great deal of scope for investment in Volume 2, where walking along fresh paths can bring not only immense satisfaction but very real profits.

VOLUME 2

It is fairly obvious that if the most popular countries are grouped into one catalogue, the others will suffer. Here the collector should remember that popularity is a fickle thing, and from time to time these disdained areas rise to prominence on the market, with consequent profit to the man who ignored the previous climate of opinion.

Israel and Vatican City are of course two such countries with an almost perennial attraction for religious reasons; such places as Laos and Korea have a good following for political reasons, while San Marino and Liechtenstein owe their popularity to speculation. For other countries no simple reason can be adduced, but this brief survey may throw some light on neglected areas as well as explain the ebb and flow of popularity elsewhere.

An important question to ask oneself here is: What is the size of the home market for these stamps? French colonial issues are highly esteemed in France, of course;

those of the former Italian colonies have a wide following in
Italy, and German ex-colonies are improving on the German
home market. The small but active Belgian and Dutch
markets swallow up their own colonial material in vast
quantities, and of course the Communist bloc offers an immense and ready-made market for issues of Russia and its
satellites, encouraged by official organizations and built up
by restrictions on the import of Western material, particularly of certain issues regarded as anti-Communist
propaganda.

The best way, therefore, to look at these stamps is by
examining the countries according to their sphere of influence. In every case the collector, having made his choice, is
not only recommended but practically ordered to acquire
immediately the standard catalogue issued in the country
where the market is strongest—the most important are Yvert
or Cérès for French Group territories, Michel for the German area, and Zumstein for Switzerland. In these books
he will find not only more realistic international market valuations (bearing in mind the conventions of pricing used)
and far more detailed information on all issues, but also lists
of stamps which do not appear in American catalogues at all.
All this, of course, is in addition to the standard advice to
join the relevant specialist society.

A young friend of mine decided many years ago to collect the stamps of Switzerland, after checking the catalogue
values in Scott's (he was very inexperienced!). Ten years
later, he has spent several thousand dollars—partly, it is
true, because of the rise in market valuations of the better
stamps which he "left until later," but mainly because he
did not discover until later the real scope of the country he
was attempting. His collection is now a fine property, but
he would have done far better right from the start if he
had found out all about it first.

France presents probably more than any one collector
could satisfactorily tackle today, and the Yvert catalogue

lists many sidelines which in themselves offer plenty of scope. Looking at the colonies, past and present, the best thing to do is to categorize them as living (still issuing stamps under the French aegis), dead (absorbed into other colonies or now using the stamps of France itself), or independent.

Dead countries like Oubangui-Chari are less popular, but at least offer the chance for completeness in the stamp issues, although the specialist will want to take them as part of the present territory, the Central African Republic. Countries which have split up into independent states outside the French area, such as French Indochina, are often collected as forerunners by specialists in the modern issues. Live countries which have achieved full independence are often very good investments, depending on other features of their development.

The live countries still counted within the French sphere offer considerable diversity in themselves; probably the two best groups are small islands (Martinique, St. Pierre and Miquelon, Réunion) and the Pacific islands of French Polynesia, New Caledonia, Wallis and Futuna, and, of course, the French-inscribed stamps of New Hebrides). All of these are recommended without reservation.

The African countries are perhaps less worthy of consideration, but the collector should take each one on its merits, considering particularly the strength of the French market and the existence of large numbers of high-value commemoratives of doubtful philatelic interest.

Germany offers blue-chip material from the old independent states; from the mixed issues of the empire; from the Nazi issues, which are currently improving; and from the modern East and West nations, which include a multitude of "Towns" issues for parts of the Russian Zone, several fine items from the French Zone, and the more run-of-the-mill Allied Occupation issues. West German issues have recently slumped due to overinvestment and poor knowledge of the market by small collectors; nevertheless, issues from 1947 to about 1954 should provide a steady investment, while later issues are reasonably cheap and are certainly attractive. Germany is likely always to be popular, but no great surprises can be expected except from the early blue chips.

East German issues have been unpopular due to the policy of blocking single values; in each set, one value is available only against purchase of larger quantities of the other values, and the greater proportion are kept for export. The custom is unethical, and undermines confidence. Berlin's issues are a political oddity and show no signs of losing popularity—but, they are subject to fluctuation through the German market.

The German colonies provide rather dull issues, but those of Samoa and New Guinea will be needed by Pacific specialists; the Marianas, Carolines, and Marshalls are now under U.S. control and use American stamps, so there is less chance of their becoming popular through the Pacific boom. If, however, the U.S. Trust Territory of the Pacific were ever given its own stamps there could well be a tremendous growth in interest in the postal history of this area; but the suggestion seems unlikely, as the U.S. Government seems keen to keep things quiet in this part of their colonial empire, presumably for fear that the United Nations might suggest internal self-government and later independence for the territory, such as they have implemented in other Pacific dependencies.

Scandinavia as a whole presents the collector with probably the most clean philatelic selection of issues in Europe. Denmark, Norway, and Sweden are all far less popular than they should be; Iceland is well supported but still offers scope for much improvement. Finland shows promise of firm and fine increases over the years, and the issues of Greenland (including the packet-post stamps) have always had a following. All these countries are well worth the consideration of the collector who does not merely want pages of gaudy modern pictorials, who is prepared to take some trouble, and who wants a long-term but assured investment property.

Switzerland is a world favorite, and it's far too late for any but the wealthy collector to come in at this stage and attempt completion. The stamps are attractive and move well, but the recent recession has shown that overinvestment does not pay. Early blue-chip material is paramount in philatelic investment, and series such as the Pro Juventutes and Pro Patrias have not yet stopped rising. But it's a big field, and because of this many collectors prefer to concentrate on the United Nations issues or the stamps of Liechtenstein—the first are good, the latter overinvested at the moment.

Italian speculation has been mentioned, and should make the collector wary. However, an attractive collection can be made of the commemorative issues, and some pre-unification issues are blue chips. But beware of speculation: it's a case of giving a dog a bad name, I'm afraid, but be warned.

San Marino and Vatican City fall into the Italian area and merit the same warnings, as to a lesser extent does Monaco in the French group, although here the strength of the French market is a safeguard. In the same way the issues of Luxembourg are supported by general European demand, and among the other pocket principalities little Andorra offers scope for the collector and investor unless events overtake my words. A final tiny state is—or was— Saar, which has had stamps under alternate French and German control over an extended period, in addition to an extensive and well-researched postal history: not recommended for the novice unless he can dig deep into his pocket.

Belgium offers a mixed picture: the early issues are sought by experts and investors alike, the later ones are bedeviled with semi-postals carrying excessively high surcharges which make them subject to the F.I.P. ban. These stamps cannot be shown at exhibitions under F.I.P. rules, and for this reason are regarded in a bad light by most collectors. The Railway issues, however, offer an interesting sideline for any collector, and are on the whole not expensive.

The Netherlands provides a wide selection of attractive and interesting stamps, scope for considerable specialization, and good market prospects—which are, however, already fulfilling themselves as I write this. Of the colonies, Curaçao (now the Antilles) and Suriname are well thought of, but the issues of Netherlands New Guinea and the Indies are under somewhat of a shadow because of their incorporation into Indonesia—far from a favorite among collectors.

Austria has always had a firm following and can be regarded on the whole as a blue-chip country but one requiring considerable expenditure to complete: the best time to start Austria was at least ten years ago! Greece is a patchy country with high and low spots; obviously the earliest Olympics issues and similar internationally popular items will never stop going up.

Portugal is a country with an interesting start, a terribly dull middle, and an interesting and promising recent history. Modern stamps are attractive and well worth taking up, but anything else is a matter of taste. Of the colonies, the various issues for Madeira and the Azores, together with the postal stationery and subsequent postal history, are well recommended for long-term interest and profit. All the colonies currently issuing stamps show excellent rises over recent years, and in view of the high prices already asked for stamps of Angola, Mozambique, and Portuguese Guinea I would recommend the interested collector to look instead at Timor and the St. Thomas and Principe islands—if he can find on-cover material!

Spain has an equally long history, with perhaps far more

investment plums in the earlier years. More recent issues have also shown astounding rises, but the Spanish Arms extended series went to rather ridiculous heights for a while, then settled down at a figure which gave the new-issue client a profit of about 120 percent over his cost! Keep a close watch on quantities printed and commercially used for all postwar items, and if you want a well-researched but still promising area try the civil-war period, with all its local issues and postal history. Of the Spanish colonies, one cannot at present say a great deal, but the more recent issues of the colonies still having their own stamps are both cheap and attractive and might be worth putting aside as a very long shot; they are, however, found in junior packets and therefore cannot be recommended for any early rise.

During the troubled times after World War I a number of petty states came into existence for limited periods. These "Neuropes" were very popular at the time, and are only now coming back into a limited interest; some collectors treat them as a group and write them up from a historical viewpoint. The group includes Allenstein, Danzig, Fiume, Marienwerder, Memel, Schleswig, and Silesia (outside the Russian group, which will be discussed later), and each can be extended in both directions by the addition of covers bearing stamps of other countries used in these areas.

The Communist bloc offers far too much for anyone to try to take it on complete. In fact, in the postwar years almost every country has issued such a surfeit of commemorative and propaganda issues that they cannot be considered seriously. Apart from Russia itself—probably the most prolific stamp-issuing country in the world but offering fringe interests in the post-1917 local and revolutionary issues, and the fascinating and highly recommended but uncatalogued Zemstvo (local council) posts—this group comprises Albania, Bulgaria, Czechoslovakia, Hungary, Poland, Rumania, and Yugoslavia.

Czech issues have always been highly regarded and are

worth considering so long as one ignores the c-t-o items. Early Hungary is fascinating but complex. The prewar issues of Poland are worth considering, as are certain later issues such as the local groszy surcharges. Yugoslavia is a much cleaner country as a result of its breaking away from Moscow, and many recent commemorative sets are appreciating nicely; the early Chainbreakers have been excessively researched, leaving little scope for further discoveries.

The many short-lived states absorbed into the Soviet Union include Armenia, Azerbaidzhan, Estonia, Ingermanland (Ingria), Latvia, Lithuania, Transcaucasia, and the Ukraine. Unfortunately there are many forgeries, fakes, and bogus stamps in this field; the collector is warned firmly off unless he has real expertise.

This necessarily brief survey of Europe closes with the issues of Turkey, which were in use over a wide area prior to 1918 and so enter into the postal history of many other countries. All are well researched and some are quite valuable, depending far more on the postmark than on the stamp. More recent issues are slightly suspect because of restrictive conditions of issue, but they are attractive and, provided they do not carry any great premium on purchase, may well turn out to be better than most tipsters seem to think at present.

Among independent countries of the old French empire in Africa we find Dahomey, Guinea, Ivory Coast, Mali, Mauritania, the Niger republic and Upper Volta. These are a mixed bag; while it can be assumed that older issues are as reliable as those of other French colonies, one must examine the catalogue for a good idea of their current "purity" and potential, if any. The same goes for other former colonial territories in Africa—Burundi, Rwanda, Congo, Somalia, and others.

With the Middle East we come to more interesting territories: Algeria, Persia, Israel, Jordan, Lebanon, Libya, Morocco, Saudi Arabia, Syria, and Tunisia. Israel is in a class of its own and needs no recommendation. Jordan, Libya, Saudi Arabia, and Syria all offer considerable interest, but as investments can only be regarded as "sleepers"—which certainly does not preclude a sudden awakening if conditions are right.

With Persia we come to the problem of forgeries, of which there are many among the earlier issues. Extreme care is advised, although modern issues may be worth putting aside. Algeria's close French connections give it a steady popularity; its investment potential looks good, as does that of Tunisia, which has produced some of the most charming—if oddball—designs ever to appear on stamps. These bear watching for their quaintness as well as for the clean philatelic policy of the country. Ethiopia is an interesting country which has known several bouts of popularity but which is currently in the doldrums—this is again a country to watch.

In Asia, Afghanistan went through a nasty agency scandal a few years back, but apart from these issues the stamps are well worth taking, particularly locally used. Tannu Tuva too suffered from agency manipulation, but recovery looks imminent; if you can find covers of any period, put them straight into the old oak chest without any qualms at all.

In the Far East we find the balance of the Volume 2 countries, and a fine mixed bag they are: China and its multitudinous local issues from the time of the Japanese invasion and the Communist takeover, Indonesia, Japan, Korea, Cambodia-Laos-Vietnam-Thailand in a tight group, and the Ryukyu Islands.

If you want a lifetime's study with a few plums and a terrific amount of nasty reprints, try China. If you want to follow the spread of U.S. influence in the area, the stamps of Taiwan, the Ryukyus, and to a lesser extent the old Indochina group will portray this very well; naturally these are the countries most collected in the United States, so you can draw the necessary conclusions about market prices.

Thailand is a real beauty of a country for the collector

and investor, but both Korea and Vietnam suffer from the exclusion of Communist issues from the catalogue, although both have seen considerable improvement so far as the listed stamps are concerned. Indonesia is currently discounted, material being cheaply available because of the collapse of the currency. Laos and Cambodia may still offer something for future years, but of the whole Far East it is Japan which shows the greatest improvement and the best chance of future profit.

The Japanese economic miracle has brought tremendous home demand for the early classics, the interesting middle issues, and the later postwar commemoratives, and I can hardly think that the trend has reached its peak by any means. However, in the last few years the policy has been to provide far larger printings of the attractive commemorative issues, and there is therefore little likelihood that they will show anything like the improvement of their predecessors. Automatic letter-sorting is now being introduced, and this has brought new regular designs; such situations are just made for the investor. In any case, almost all the stamps of Japan are attractive, and so long as you do not get mixed up with the early forgeries (of which there are many) you should find the country both interesting and attractive, as well as a good investment even at this late stage in the boom.

CONCLUSION

This has been of necessity a brief and condensed survey. The intention has not been to pick out every good country, or even to damn every bad one, but to serve as an exercise in how to interpret the catalogue. As the years pass, the policy of some countries will change, and popularity will come and go, but the principles governing philatelic investment do not change.

NEW FIELDS

THERE IS NO need to restrict yourself to certain countries or to straightforward stamps and postal markings. In fact, it is not advisable to be so singleminded, as profit and pleasure often lie in diversity.

Postal stationery—the printed postcards, envelopes, and letter-cards with imprinted stamps—were once collected equally with stamps. Unfortunately, the tendency was to cut out the imprinted stamp and throw the rest away, a practice which nowadays is, to say the least, frowned upon. Scott's catalogue lists U.S. material of this type, and Higgins & Gage are now producing a loose-leaf catalogue of worldwide postal stationery, taking in such newer forms as aerograms and airgraphs. Prices are still ludicrously low for most of this material, especially when one considers the probable remaining quantities of mint pieces in dealers' and collectors' hands, and all have an assured future.

The Higgins & Gage catalogue is being corrected and added to in the process of publication; earlier parts revealed some major omissions and deficiencies. It will repay the interested collector to keep an eye on all future parts with a view to updating and amending the pages referring to his own countries. It is difficult to say whether airpost stationery and other material of this type should be collected mint or used, and as some of the commemorative items exist with special postmarks it is advisable to make the scope of your collection as wide as possible, secure in the knowledge that if at a later date you decide to take only mint or only used items you will be able to dispose of the balance at a favorable price.

Postage-due labels have for some reason never been as popular with collectors as postage stamps; there is no logical reason for this as they are true postal items, and a collection of covers bearing these labels would be a desirable adjunct to any collection. Some countries do not have postage-dues, but use ordinary stamps to collect unpaid fees; covers showing such usage should certainly be included in your collection.

Official stamps have been issued by some countries; others, such as Australia and Papua, have used normal stamps perforated across the design with the letters "OS" or a similar inscription. Again the investor is recommended to ignore popular opinion and incorporate a good showing of these into his collection, particularly on official covers. In both cases the mint stamps should also be taken up.

First-flight covers have always had a steady following, although the craze of the thirties has now abated. This field is plagued by a multitude of blatantly commercial and philatelic items for some countries, but provided the collection is not swamped in these items but contains examples of covers from all the *important* early flights, it is a firm investment and a most interesting and attractive adjunct to any country collection.

Islands have always received the greater part of their mail by sea, and many special markings exist which tell the story of the sea posts. There are also a large number of unofficial ship markings which, while adding color and interest, have no specifically philatelic significance. However, a good representative collection of these postal markings, with particular emphasis on the early official "Paquebot" and "Ship Letter" marks, will be an excellent investment and will add a new dimension to your understanding of the postal history of the country. The Pacific in particular offers immense scope for the collector, and this is one area where even "philatelic" covers have a degree of acceptance in the absence of other mail from some sources.

I have already mentioned the Zemstvo posts of Russia; there are other "locals" which, although not accepted for listing by the major catalogues, offer a fine field for the investor. Prime among these are perhaps the "Interim Period" issues of Palestine-Israel, used between the end of the British Mandate postal services and the establishment of the State of Israel's official posts. There are catalogues which list these issues, although their pricing is very much a matter of opinion and there are gaps in most of the lists. This is not the place to set out on a full discussion of these interesting items, but including as they do armored-car posts, bicycle mails, Haganah illegal army posts, siege mail from Jerusalem, and many other oddities, they provide endless interest and attraction for the investor with a fair amount of cash to spend.

Probably the best way to pick up this material is at postal auctions, especially at those held in Israel, and careful study of these auction catalogues will provide a good picture of relative scarcity and values. The Mosden catalogue has much valuable information, although it is not comprehensive and puts perhaps too much emphasis on mint examples.

I make this last point because there is a tremendous quantity of forgeries in this field. Blatantly philatelic covers are in the majority, but even these are collectable so long as they can be authenticated; it is far harder to verify the bona fides of mint stamps than of covers. A point in favor of taking up these fascinating Interim issues is that, in view of the ridiculously small quantities of covers which exist, prices are still very low. As a rough guide to the newcomer, covers may cost anything from $2 to $200, depending on the stamps and postal markings, but further international recognition, especially by the editors of the standard catalogues, would change the whole face of the market overnight.

Local posts also functioned in many European countries and towns in the middle of the last century. Depending on conditions of issue and use, the attitude of the official postal administrations at the time, and the overall popularity of the countries concerned, these may be found to be valuable, reasonable, or ludicrously cheap. The warning here is against accepting *any* label as a valid local post without further corroboration. For example, labels of many offshore islands of Britain have recently been condemned in no uncertain terms by the British Philatelic Association and the Philatelic Traders' Society, and all these items must be offered for sale in Britain only under the title of "local carriage labels" or "local issues"; the word "stamps" cannot be used in their descriptions, a stipulation upheld by the responsible U.S. philatelic press as well. Issues of the islands of Lundy and Herm, and of the Commodore Shipping Company, are certainly acceptable as "fringe" collections, but none is recommended for early investment improvement.

When one comes to the local issues of the United States, the infallible guide is Scott's Specialized catalogue. There are many bogus issues and forgeries, but the genuine items are all clearly set out and priced in this invaluable work. Scott's catalogue also lists revenues; these stamps, usually referred to in other countries as fiscals, have a very limited following outside the United States. The main thing the collector should keep in mind is that philately concerns itself with postage stamps and markings and that anything which is non-postal is of minority interest.

Postal issues of the United States include the categories of postal stationery, airpost stamps and stationery, special delivery and airpost special delivery, booklet stamps and panes, coil stamps and rolls, carriers' stamps, certified mail stamps, issues of the Confederate states and postmasters' provisionals and general issues, local stamps, newspaper and periodical stamps, official stamps, postage-dues, parcel-post stamps and dues, registration stamps—plenty here to occupy even the most avid collector.

On the other hand, Christmas seals, telegraph stamps, savings and war savings stamps, and the many revenue issues produced for various fiscal purposes are all non-postal. They nevertheless have a small but assured following, and prices of some items do tend to move upward, although much of this movement is due to inflation and to brief spasms of popularity caused by the issue of a new catalogue or specialized study which brings more collectors into the field. Popularity is seldom based on logic, but looking at the hobby from a world-wide viewpoint—as the careful investor must always strive to do—it seems fair to say that these items will never have the popularity that real postage stamps have.

A final word on this subject: if you are offered, at a very reasonable price, a selection of the fiscal stamps of *any* country in which you are interested, there is no harm in taking them up—if only so that you can claim to be one of the few collectors to own such material!

At the risk, however, of upsetting some American collectors and dealers, I must say that I have never been able to understand the demand for Christmas seals. These serve absolutely no purpose, either for postage or for revenue, and, unlike those of South Africa and Denmark, are not even sold by the Post Office. It is the beguilement with such ephemera as these which causes the American collector to be held up as a figure of scorn abroad.

International Reply Coupons are regular postal emissions, printed to an agreed international design and often showing short-lived provisional surcharges, additional franking with postage stamps, and other local points of interest, in addition to postmarks which are often of considerable interest. It is the Israel and the U.S. specialist who tend to take these up, and they are listed in the specialist catalogues of these two countries.

On the fringes of philately are the collectors of registration labels and of recorded delivery, express post, and airmail etiquettes (labels indicating a paid service with no indication of denomination). Certainly these are susceptible to study, but should not be removed from covers: only when allied with the stamps and postal markings proper to their use can they tell a story.

Returning to adhesive postage stamps: I have mentioned that modern British regulars (and, incidentally, the three low values of the Silver Jubilee set of 1935) are issued in booklets in which a proportion of the stamps showed sideways or inverted watermarks. It must not be forgotten that the booklets themselves are often of considerable premium value over their contents, and are listed in many catalogues. There has always been a tendency among collectors to "explode" booklets, spreading out the stamp and interleaving panes on the album page; while this creates a coherent display it detracts from the investment value, and complete booklets can easily be mounted (though not displayed) by making two vertical slits in the album page and sliding the book cover through these. In any case, exploded or not, booklets form an essential part of any specialized collection and are also worthwhile investments, especially from out-of-the-way countries where quantities are small.

Stamps are occasionally found with a "Specimen" overprint, and these are often rejected by collectors as being in some way "spoiled"; for this reason they demand far lower prices than their scarcity would otherwise lead one to expect. I have mentioned the Australian "Specimen sets," the higher values of which are overprinted in this way; these should not be confused with other "Specimens" as they are on sale generally to the public at a fraction of face value. Nevertheless, many of these are fast attaining to higher prices and they should never be discarded as uncollectable.

The reason for the existence of the real "Specimen" stamps of the United States and of the British colonial area

—which are found overprinted in various typefaces and, in later years, pin-perforated into the face of the stamp—lies in the requirement that copies of all newly issued stamps be supplied to the Universal Postal Union for distribution to member nations as a guarantee of their validity, and for file at the U.P.U. headquarters in Berne. It is these stamps which have subsequently come on the market from various sources, and since the original quantities distributed were in earlier days some eight hundred sets and in later years (up to 1947, when pin-perforating ceased) little more than four hundred sets, it will be appreciated that they are extremely scarce and whenever offered should be snapped up!

It should be made clear that not all colonial issues were so treated, and that "Specimen" or similar overprints on stamps of foreign countries are often applied for quite different reasons: for example, German stamps marked "Muster" are issued in small quantities to the press for publicity purposes, Spanish-language stamps overprinted "Muestra" are made available to the trade for advertising, and Japanese "Mihon" overprints are issued to schools. All these have a specialized following and all have a premium value, but they do not fall into the same category as the U.S. and colonial U.P.U. items.

Investigation of the methods by which stamps are produced leads one back ultimately to the original artist's drawings and essays, and to proof impressions of various types. All are extremely scarce and valuable, and for many countries are unobtainable. Proofs which may be acquired, and which are recognized by specialist catalogues, are those for stamps printed by the French Atelier de Fabrication des Timbres-Poste in Paris. Here "artists' proofs" and "de luxe proofs" are pulled in limited quantities for record and presentation purposes, and these come frequently on the market. They tell an important part of the story of stamp design and merit a place in any collection.

Also produced, and listed in French catalogues, are imperforate stamps, some in monocolor and others in issued colors or other combinations. These, like the gummed presentation sheets which exist for some issues, are now "collector bait" and, despite their following in France and the United States, cannot be regarded as essential to the production of the finished stamps. Originally, these imperforate "color trials" were made to help the authorities decide which colors should finally be employed, but they are now made in quite unnecessary quantities even where colors are known from the start!

The main thing for the investor to remember is the difference between these items and their relative scarcity.

Artists' proofs rarely exist in more than twenty copies; they are usually in black but do exist in other colors, and are often of considerable value. Progress proofs may exist where a single design is to be used for several values; the first stage is a proof lacking any face value, this being inserted at a later stage to several transfer dies from the original. De luxe proofs are usually on stiff paper and exist in quantities of perhaps two hundred to four hundred copies. These are sought after but obviously far less scarce than artists' proofs, although popular themes such as the French Arts series may cause some to rise to very high figures on the market.

Imperforate stamps are made in strips, usually of five impressions in a number of colors with a full-color combination at the end; separation of the individual impressions lowers their value. Presentation sheets are also usually imperforate and on gummed paper of a quality similar to that of the issued stamps.

Proofs of countries outside the French group come in many forms, and there are often forgeries and unofficial reprints to contend with. The specialist is strongly advised to read up on his own country, then when such items turn up *and they are genuine* he should acquire them at once.

A final word on sidelines. Never be put off by the self-appointed expert who tells you that material of this or that type will never be worth anything. If he persists, offer to buy from him all he may have and any he can acquire for you at a reasonable price—you may well be surprised at his reaction! If you are told that certain material cannot be found, that nobody has it, this is a green light for you to go ahead and search hard. Whatever the sideline, if it has any real connection with philately it will one day become popular, more valuable, and sought after. Ignore current climates of opinion and get in first.

F.D.C.'S

AND

MAX-CARDS

THE FIRST-DAY COVER—an envelope bearing a stamp or stamps postmarked with the first day of issue of the emission—has a long and honorable history: f.d.c.'s of the Penny Black are avidly sought and command considerable premiums. For most issues up to about 1925 they are extremely scarce, as few collectors saw any special value in obtaining them and most of those remaining were sent to relatives and friends with comments such as "I thought you'd like to see the pretty (or ugly) new stamps that came out here today."

The provision of specially prepared first-day covers, with commemorative inscriptions or cachets, started at different dates in different countries. In Britain even the issues of Edward VIII in 1936 are usually found on plain envelopes with a manuscript notation, but the following year brought many dull but recognizable Coronation f.d.c.'s onto the market. In the postwar years the covers became more and more ornate, with large multicolored designs which in many cases quite killed the effect of the stamps themselves; this custom is to be deprecated, but there is no denying that it caters to the lowest common denominator of collector demand.

Earlier f.d.c.'s, if only by virtue of their scarcity, are good property, but the more recent confections serve only to provide the collector with fine-used copies of the stamps, often bearing a special one-day postmark which, depending on popularity and changes in taste, may or may not keep its premium value in years to come.

So far as modern U.S. f.d.c.'s are concerned, the problem is bedeviled by two separate considerations. First, many different unofficial designs exist—far more so than in other countries, and some costing far more than any of the attached stamps. Production of ornate cachets does not add to the value of a cover in any philatelic sense, and as a result most of these items are soon discounted. It is the early covers, where scarcity and not design is the prime factor, which bring higher prices, and those which can be recommended as cast-iron investments are relatively few. Second, U.S. commemoratives are generally of low face value and exist in used condition in massive quantities; even high-value regular stamps are plentiful in commercially used condition in comparison with figures for foreign countries. From these two factors it can be seen that a first-day cover has only limited collector interest and, certainly for recent years, carries little premium over the stamps themselves, which have but small potential.

For foreign countries, there are other factors to be considered. First, the covers may be issued by the postal administration itself, in which case they are genuine postal emissions. Second, the face value of the stamps may be quite high and supplies of ordinarily used examples relatively scarce. Third, a stable collector interest exists for some countries, which will always give their covers a market value.

For small islands there is always a demand for first-day covers, since there is so little mail of any sort that even f.d.c.'s are apt to be scarce. But the real value of such a cover lies not in its being an impressive production replete with ornamentation and special markings, well thought out in advance, but where it bears an unannounced provisional issue which appeared unexpectedly and caught the trade sleeping!

A final important consideration here is in the answer to the question: Does a recognized catalogue exist for f.d.c.'s of the country concerned? If it does, then this will in itself encourage their collection, increase demand (particularly for earlier items issued before the appearance of the catalogue), and so improve their investment potential.

The maximum card is a much more recent innovation. It comprises a picture postcard, with a stamp having a connected theme affixed to the picture side and postmarked with a relevant cancellation, preferably on the date of issue. The earliest British maximum card I have seen is a 1d. stamp of the 1929 Postal Union Congress, attached to a sepia picture postcard of London Bridge and tied with a first-day circular handstamp of the nearest London office. When I was offered it in 1966 at 30 cents, I let it pass, but I may come to regret my action: as a souvenir of the congress it is doubtless of interest, and by virtue of its scarcity it may well turn out to be of value.

Max-cards in the United States suffer from the same disability as first-day covers: the production is costly and far outstrips the value of the stamp. Also, many such items are produced solely for the stamp issue, whereas the organization concerned with the regularization of maximum cards, Les Maximaphiles Français, stresses that the particular postcard should already be in existence, feeling that the greater part of the fun lies in finding such cards and having them prepared in time to gain the required special postmark.

Foreign countries, ranging from France to Chile and from Switzerland to Algeria, have produced official or private maximum cards for many years, at least back into the forties, but the cards have been rather slow to catch on. Most collectors have been deterred by the high prices asked for what is obviously a philatelic item produced in quantity at no great cost. The British postal authorities do not approve of maximum cards and have refused to cancel stamps on the picture side of postcards unless the picture takes up only a portion of the space and the address appears on the same side. This regulation has now been abolished, and similar

strictures do not apply in foreign countries, where the cards
are cancelled and handed back across the counter to the
customer.

Recent issues of maximum cards to appear on the market
in Britain have been prepared by a variety of subterfuges,
the main one being to prepare a card of massive size, the
blank portion bearing the address, which is then clipped off
before sale. This rather shoddy arrangement should not com-
mend itself to the sensible collector, but with the regularization of the practice there is bound to be a greater demand
for such items, so if you really feel that your collection needs
such material, buy it as it appears and just put it aside.

YOUR

COLLECTION

MANY THOUSANDS of dollars' worth of mint sheets of stamps have been rendered valueless overnight by carelessness, stupidity, or ignorance. Untold quantities of single stamps in albums and stockbooks have been ruined in the same way. An important fact which so many people overlook is that paper has weight.

Stamps are fragile things, and mint stamps are even more fragile because of their gum. They can get stuck together, stuck to album pages, or even stuck in stockbook pockets by pressure, heat, or dampness.

Stamps should be aired regularly to prevent mold or rust and to avoid adhesion. The ordinary collector who loves to look at his stamps and show them to his friends suffers far less from the effects of storage because his collection is aired as he pores over the pages. The investor often forgets this, and his precious material lies locked up in drawers or bank vaults, losing value with every day that passes.

Keep your stamps in a cool, dry room. A well-used lounge or dining room is quite suitable, so long as no cooking takes place there and the heating is kept at a sensible level; the coming and going of people will help keep the air circulating and avoid extremes of temperature.

Stockbooks and albums should always be stored on end, and never pressed too tightly together; stamps and covers should never be sealed in polythene or kept in airtight containers. Mint sheets and large blocks should always be stored in special sheet stockbooks, stood on end and properly braced but not under pressure. Every part of the collection should be looked over regularly and rearranged in different order on the shelf.

All these notes, of course, refer to collecting in temperate climates. The investor faced with keeping his treasures in an exceptionally hot or humid climate will have to take special steps to safeguard them: mint stamps can be brushed with fine talc to keep them from sticking together, and airtight containers may be essential during the wet season. However, whenever the climate permits he should bring out every piece and examine it carefully for danger signs.

If all this sounds over-fussy, remember that condition is all-important in philately, and that the major reason for the high value of many pieces is simply that they survived—so many others have been damaged or destroyed over the years. Stamps may well be regarded as money in the bank, but they can't be treated as if they were banknotes or stock certificates.

When you mount mint stamps, apply to the hinge—and *only* to the hinge—the very least amount of moisture needed. Moisture which seeps out onto the stamp will stick it to the page. Use only the very best peelable hinges—anything else is a waste of your money, and it would be folly to spoil a valuable stamp because of a difference in cost of perhaps 10 cents per 1,000 hinges.

"Protective mounts" have become popular in recent years because of the "unmounted-mint" demand. These strips are certainly a boon, as they will protect delicate stamps from rubbing and creasing when the album pages are turned. Even stamps in stockbooks can be damaged if they slip out or become entangled with the protective cellophane sheets, so a stamp in a protective mount placed inside a stockbook pocket is less an oddity than one might imagine.

However, we have already seen that with the increase in

illicit regumming, the primacy of the unmounted-mint specimen may be slowly coming to an end, and the experts are
united in insisting that a well-mounted stamp is as acceptable as one in "unhinged" condition. It is certain that no real
rarity will be faulted for the lack of untouched gum, so long
as it is undamaged and unthinned.

Pure investment stocks—full mint sheets and the like—
may never be intended for incorporation into a collection at
all, but used simply as a means of turning a profit at a later
date. However, the real focus of any collection is the album
leaf, and this involves writing up, mounting, and some consideration of display in telling the story of the stamps and
covers. The story may be historical, postal, geographical,
topical, or technical, and it must be presented logically,
written up briefly and knowledgeably (and tidily), and
illustrated with the right material tastefully presented and
carefully mounted. There are many good primers on arrangement, and with thought and practice the collector will be
able to evolve his own style and approach.

The sensible investor will create a collection which is
personal, meaningful, and attractive—and as complete as he
can manage. He will spend time on research and study and
will incorporate the fruits of this in his write-up. He will
ensure that his collection contains as many of the "plums" of
the country as he can afford, so long as each contributes
something to the story. Such a collection, adorned if required
with postal notices, maps, or other collateral material (which
must be strictly philatelic and not merely added for show),
will eventually merit display to specialist society meetings,
thus establishing the owner as somewhat of an expert. If at
this stage he can write articles or a monograph or, better
still, produce a catalogue of a previously unlisted field, he
will be well on the way to making his own collection well
known.

The next step is to exhibit, first at local society competi-
tions, later at regional and national levels. Given time, care,

and cash, the collection may one day merit entry into international exhibitions. Such a collection becomes a "name" collection, nationally and even internationally recognized, and as such it will automatically acquire a higher value when offered for sale.

A further reason for exhibiting is that it puts the collector in touch with other dealers and collectors, who then become aware of his wants. Reassured by his standing, they will offer him better pieces, putting material his way which he might otherwise never see at all. So he gains all around!

I have several times stressed "completeness." This is, of course, a relative term—real completeness would entail owning every copy of every item in the world! But any collection should be complete so far as the catalogues will take you; it should be as broadly based in its postal history and sidelines as possible, without glaring gaps which will be obvious at a glance to the expert eye. It is only after this stage is passed that the acquisition of additional copies of rarities becomes sensible; possession of such "international gold" material then has a prestige value which may be given almost as much weight as that allowed for the work and study involved in the entire collection.

But one must learn to walk before he can run, and at the local and national levels, where one is given only a few frames to fill, it is hard work and expertise that count. At the international level you will be required to enter your whole collection for consideration, and it will be upon the entire picture that you will be judged.

For the less wealthy collector, who cannot see himself aspiring to the heights of international exhibiting, I must make a few important points. First of all, if you pursue your investment collection skillfully, picking up every bargain you are offered in your field even if it strains your resources, and if you learn how to sell at the best time to the best advantage, you will find that the profits you make as you go along will amply feed your main collection, taking you up to national level without too much difficulty in a few years or so.

Once you become known, other experts will be keen to help you, and your progress thus becomes faster. It is the secret collector, the man who will never show at his local society, who has the hardest task. So long as you show yourself willing to contribute actively to a specialist society—if not by research then at least by serving on a committee—you will make worthwhile friends just when and where you need them. In time they will come to need you, too!

As you climb the philatelic tree, your expenditures will rise slowly and imperceptibly from cents to dollars to hundreds of dollars for a single item, without your feeling the strain, for you will be cushioned from the rising costs by the increased market value of your investment material, which can be shed at will along the path.

We all have to start at the bottom: those who rise to the top do so because they have studied, learned, and made use of their knowledge. To do this you must know your stamps, and must understand the trade and how it functions.

PRICING

THE NEW COLLECTOR is often puzzled to find in one issue of a philatelic paper the same stamps offered by several dealers but at different prices. They may even be new issues, where one would expect close agreement, yet prices may vary by 5 cents on a 50-cent item. There seems to be no single market price for anything, even after one discounts the obvious "loss leaders" inserted in advertisements merely to encourage orders for other, more expensive items.

The "catalogue value" is often quoted as a standard, but the collector soon finds that there are many catalogues, all with different prices, and that none of these seems to bear any direct connection with the various market prices. Some catalogues, he discovers, are not backed by any stocks but are the editors' estimated market valuations; others are based on market prices at a given date; still others are produced by dealers and purport to quote their current selling prices.

The Yvert & Tellier catalogue, used throughout the French-speaking world, is often accepted as a standard by dealers, who offer to supply at a straight 60 or 70 percent of Yvert prices. Yet the Cérès and Thiaude catalogues are also printed in France and their valuations differ, often markedly, from Yvert. Both Zumstein's and Müller's catalogues are produced in Switzerland, and they too differ.

How is the collector to form any real idea of the value
of his collection and the right price to pay for what he
needs?

The collector comes to believe that in the last analysis
there is no such thing as a *real* price for a stamp, and here he
is correct: there is only the market price, with all its fluctuations and with the different valuations given it by dealers,
depending on whether or not they have large stocks for sale.
Moreover, this generalized market price can change from
day to day or remain static for years.

The stamp market is thus wide open to anyone who
wishes to buy and sell. It has no strict organization, no closed
shop, no brokers or intermediaries who fix prices. A dealer in
a country town may happily exist selling stamps to his clients
at prices bearing little or no relation to the current market
position. Even in New York's Nassau Street, the center of the
American stamp market, there is little or no price fixing, and
neither client nor dealer wants to see such controls introduced; in any case, they would be unworkable.

It is in his interpretation of the catalogue valuations and
in his observation of the day-to-day movements of the market that the market tipster produces his tips. By learning a
little more about these things than the average collector
knows, the investor can make use of his own observations
and deductions to make money for him.

First of all, every dealer is faced with different problems.
Generally speaking, a large firm has a high overhead and
must spend a lot on purely "prestige" advertising to maintain
its name before the collecting world. It must also buy and
sell in large quantities in order to keep solvent, and in these
transactions it has quite a definite effect on the market. If
the large dealer is also a cataloguer, he may find that his
own catalogue quotations affect the prices at which he is
offered material, and this can be a dangerous tool in his
hands. On the other hand, where the market outflanks him,
his catalogue may become useless and discounted, with con-

sequent effect on his ability to supply stamps or to sell them.

In the middle range are the many firms with small staffs and having rent to pay, tax payments to make, and a precarious reputation to maintain for service and efficiency. These may vary from expensive shops on Nassau Street to large but less costly ones in the suburbs or out of town.

There are many postal-business firms, employing a staff but not having the overhead incurred in running a shop. They must advertise far more widely, and their offers must be in effect detailed price lists. They may also produce lists for sending out to their regular clientele; such lists are expensive to produce and to distribute, and are time-consuming to compile.

Then there is the man with no staff except perhaps a long-suffering wife, running a small shop in a small town. He will depend largely on a small but faithful local clientele, which he may enlarge by advertising for postal business. His is a complex existence, since he must have adequate stocks available in the shop for all the likely calls of his regulars, in addition to a postal record system and perhaps extra stocks at home.

At the bottom of the scale is the part-time, postal-only, one-man-band—the "kitchen-table dealer" with small stocks, a small mailing list, and practically no overhead. He has another job to feed himself and his family, and he probably has an urge to take up dealing full time if the cards fall right. He can, of course, operate on a far smaller profit margin than larger dealers, but his sources of material are limited and he is almost certainly undercapitalized.

If the small dealer could supply all one's wants to order, there would be little or no reason for the larger firms to exist. But when one adds up the collector's expenditure in time, postage, money-order fees, and the duplication of effort in contacting a dozen or more small dealers, it becomes obvious that the larger dealer, with his more diversified stock and better contacts, is better able to serve his clients. His prices will on the whole be considerably higher than those of the small dealer, but by virtue of his "name" and prestige he is offered more and better material, he can afford to pay more for it and so replenish his stocks more thoroughly, and he offers *service*.

All this helps us to understand the wide spectrum of prices seen in any issue of a magazine. But it does not explain, for example, how one dealer can afford to advertise to *buy* stamps at a higher price than another is offering them for sale. It is here that the problem of time-lag enters the picture.

Even weekly stamp journals have a "copy date" two weeks before publication date; this means that advertisements (complete with prices, of course) must be in the hands of the printers two weeks before they are printed; for monthly magazines the copy date is even earlier. Advertisement prices are, therefore, partly based on stocks and purchase prices in effect weeks prior to publication, and partly on an estimate of market movements—which at times is comparable to reading a crystal ball. The dealer with wide contacts will know of certain market movements before his humbler brethren do, and even days can count here.

Thus the small dealer may find that by the time his advertisement appears he has exhausted his stocks and is unable to replace them even at his previous *selling* price; on the other hand, if he has taken a chance and pushed up his prices too high he will have few takers, and so the cost of the advertisement is lost.

This brings us to another important point: an advertisement is *not legally* an offer to sell (or, as the case may be, to buy); it is merely an invitation to the reader to make an offer of business to the advertiser. And this need not be accepted by the dealer, either at the prices quoted or indeed at any price at all. Of course, the dealer who consistently refuses, or is unable to do business on the basis of his ad-

vertisements, will not last long, but the reader should understand clearly that he cannot attempt to enforce the
conditions of a legal agreement on the basis of an advertisement. This explains why the dealer whose advertised
prices are high will often do better business than his cheaper
colleagues—the collecting public has come to recognize his
firm as reliable, and they are prepared to pay more in order
to assure themselves of getting the material offered.

The reader should tread very warily when a dealer advertises both buying and selling prices for the same material,
especially if they are both on the high side. It is not un-
heard of for a dealer to quote unrealistically high buying
prices, on the basis of which he has no intention of doing
business, in order to cajole the reader into buying from him
at his equally high selling prices. This warning applies only
to a small number of firms, and again they do not as a rule
last long, for as soon as this trick becomes really obvious
they find themselves barred from the pages of every reputable magazine. However, for as long as their advertisements
appear they can seriously upset the market in a limited range
of material, and may well damage the readers' confidence in
dealers and in the investment potential of the items
concerned.

So we see that the catalogue is far from being an infallible guide to the market, although in certain limited
ranges the collector can learn to buy at a fixed percentage
of the prices shown for certain countries in certain catalogues, secure in the knowledge that he will not be seriously
swindled by acting in this way. However, it should be remembered that where a catalogue quotation is unrealistic,
the material has a habit of disappearing "under the counter"
until quotations can be modified! The only real guide to
the market is the market itself, and this can be observed
satisfactorily only by visiting a large number of dealers every
week; but few collectors can afford to do this in person,
and the only solution lies in studying one of the *weekly*

stamp journals, which closely mirror the state of the market.

A final point for the keen collector: although it is expensive to keep in permanent contact with a large number of dealers, it often pays off in the long run to do so, as single lots—often unrepeatable—of material in your field may then be offered to you for first refusal, which otherwise you would never see. As soon as you aspire to more specialized material, you should ensure that your name is listed with every dealer in your field. Without this you have little chance of seeing much of the scarcer material you need.

TURNOVER

IF THESE STAMPS are so highly spoken of, an investor may ask, why is the dealer prepared to sell them? Why doesn't he hold on and make a bigger profit for himself?

The answer lies in capitalization. Few dealers can afford to buy material other than for immediate, or at least speedy, turnover and may well regard any material which does not turn over in, say, three months as being wasted money. The dealer is in business to turn over as large stocks as possible, as rapidly as possible, at the smallest possible mark-up consistent with solvency. In this way a small amount of capital can be invested and reinvested over and over.

There are, of course, exceptions to this: many dealers have one small area in which they consider themselves experts and may maintain private collections which they will not consider selling at any price—or so they say! They may be prepared to buy almost anything good which is offered to them in this specialist area, to salt away for future improvement. But it is a dangerous practice for any dealer to start—there is always the temptation to take more and more from his stock to feed his private collection, which may cause considerable financial difficulty in the future.

In the field of postal history there are a few dealers who are prepared to hold on to vast stocks against minimal turnover; they can do so because their income is adequate and they are absolutely assured that with every passing year their holdings become more valuable. But these are the exceptions. To the average dealer the only thing of importance is turnover, and this means constant purchases to feed his stocks, which are always being depleted as rapidly as possible.

One further point: a dealer finding himself with large quantities of unsalable material may offer it for sale *through the trade* at well below current wholesale prices, just to realize something on it. But he will not make such offers in the collectors' magazines, as this might upset the market and would certainly cause considerable ill will in the trade; the action could cost him useful contacts, and he might in effect find himself an outcast. The "kitchen-table dealer," on the other hand, can make occasional cut-price offers, since he relies less on the goodwill of the professionals; his stocks, however, are likely to be very small and so the effect of his offers on the market price will be negligible. As far as the investor is concerned, the major point is that he will probably not be able to obtain through such occasional sources sufficient material to make the effort worthwhile.

SELLING

CAREFUL INVESTMENT BUYING is useless unless you know how and where to sell. Mint-sheet investments require a different sales technique from the specialized collection or the simple stamp collection, while single rare items will probably provide a larger profit if they are offered for sale separately.

The first thing to realize is that in any stamp collection a sizable proportion of the stamps will have little or no resale value; these are the items catalogued at, say, less than 10 cents each, and a dealer's handling charges and storage costs make it uneconomical for him to buy them at all. He will accept such material as part of a good collection, and will sell the stamps once they are in his stock, although he knows that this sort of material is available in packets at about five stamps for a penny.

A smaller proportion of stamps, those catalogued from about 10 cents to 50 cents each, will realize only a small fraction of the catalogue value from sale to a dealer, unless they are in full sets, in which case he will be prepared to pay a higher figure. Only a fair quantity of higher-value stamps in a general or one-country collection will prompt the average dealer to make an offer commensurate with the amount you have expended on it. As already mentioned, if your collection contains any real plums you will be well advised to take these out and offer them separately.

161

The specialist collector who has built up personal contacts with dealers over the years will of course approach
them when he decides to sell his collection. There is no
guarantee that the dealer will take it, or that he will offer
a high price for it, but there is a strong likelihood that he
will do so, since he will no doubt have other specialist clients
interested in the material.

The specialist will also have many contacts in the collecting world, through his membership in specialist societies.
Many of these run "exchange packets" through which material can be sold, or may hold private auctions; the bids are
high as a rule, since members are all enthusiasts and know
that they are bidding against other experts. In any case, he
may know that certain members are searching for some of
the items he is selling, and a simple letter will then do the
trick.

Any collector or investor can advertise his material for
sale in a collector's magazine. Before placing the advertisement he should ask himself which of the journals will offer
him the best market, and whether the cost of the advertisement is commensurate with the amount of material he can
expect to sell. Application to the advertising managers of
the journals will give him some information to work on, and
a careful study of other advertisements will provide a fair
idea of how best to offer what he has, how many items he
can reasonably fit into a given space, and what prices are
currently being asked for similar material.

A large advertisement will sell more material per square
inch than a smaller one; this is a simple matter of readership
impact. An offer to send a list on request will produce a far
smaller response than listing the items in the advertisement
itself. A cramped, cluttered layout will attract far less attention than one which "wastes" space to give a clearer effect.
On the other hand, if stocks are large and the investor plans
a lengthy campaign, then the size of the advertisement becomes of much less import—it is its regular appearance

which provides long-term results because prospective buyers see the insertion in each issue. Here obviously it is immediacy and frequency which count, and thus a weekly magazine will offer advantages over a less frequent one.

Please do not imagine that just because you advertise you will necessarily sell! In planning an advertisement, always include certain items which you *know* are popular and which will provide you with sufficient profit (not just income, but sheer profit) to pay for the advertisement. All sales of other material are then cost-free. The art of advertising is a complex one, and the quickest way to learn it is to observe the displays of successful firms. Remember that your insertion is competing on unequal terms with every larger one in that issue, and on equal terms with every one of the same size: don't spoil your chances by poor presentation and badly chosen material, so that your ad is outshone by even the smaller insertions!

Many collectors and investors feel unsure about pricing. Nobody will give you advice on what price to ask: it is your material, you know what you paid for it, and you must decide what you think you can get for it. When you take your material to a dealer he will rarely make you an offer: he will ask your price and then accept or reject it; he may or may not make you a counter-offer. If you want him to appraise your material, he may charge for this service; you must expect to pay for his time and expertise. If he buys your collection, he will of course waive his appraisal fee.

A collector should be willing to sell some items at a loss in order to buy a stamp he really needs but cannot afford. This is unlikely to be the case if he advertises, as the delay between copy date and eventual sale may be so long as to defeat the purpose of the cheap offer. In any case, remember that an advertisement offering items far below the current market value may lead to a deluge of orders, with consequent additional cost in returning remittances.

Obviously as a collector your overhead is lower than a

dealer's, and if you have bought wisely and are selling at the right time you may stand to make a considerable profit. But do not be *too* greedy—your name is likely to be unknown to readers and therefore you cannot expect to make large sales at current retail prices. A fair idea is to pitch your prices about 10 percent below retail levels and impose a restriction on the length of time your offer is open: with a weekly magazine you might perhaps state in your advertisement "Offer for two weeks only." This is the average "life" of such an advertisement, and the restriction imparts a feeling of urgency which may bring a better and speedier response.

Remember that in placing an advertisement you are declaring yourself a dealer: you will be expected to provide adequate service and to adhere to the provisions of the various laws governing conditions of sale.

AUCTIONS

FEW COLLECTORS seem to approach the auction room, or even to apply for catalogues of postal auctions, until they have reached a certain level in collecting. This is a pity, as contrary to their belief, auction buying can offer as much to the sensible beginner as to the more experienced investor.

There are auctions where any lot valued at less than $50 is unusual and where a single item may be valued at hundreds or thousands of dollars. But there are many auctions offering smaller lots and single items at prices from $2, and it is here that the collector can often pick up material at far below market prices.

The major auctioneers, with world-wide reputations and clientele, are offered valuable and scarce material to sell; their catalogues go on subscription to thousands of collectors and dealers. Really good properties, probably unobtainable elsewhere, will excite considerable interest, reaching perhaps far higher prices in this way than they would realize elsewhere. These may be the happy hunting-grounds of the "international gold" specialist, but even here many unconsidered crumbs can fall to the watchful and careful bidder of modest means.

Smaller firms, turning out cheaply mimeographed lists—often well padded with the auctioneer's own material offered at auction in hopes of quicker sale and higher prices—also offer material from private vendors. Prices realized may well be quite low, since the clientele is small. In such auctions one should bid with care, as it is an unfortunate but undeniable fact that a small number of these firms, which operate from a private address and are not supervised in the way that the big public auctions are by their clients, may take the highest bid and not the "next step" over the second-highest bid, as is the custom.

However, real bargains turn up with remarkable regularity in these small auctions, mainly when a collector or investor has decided to sell out quickly without going to the trouble of advertising, or does not want the public recognition which an advertisement will bring.

Smaller auctions are particularly useful for acquiring unpopular material: in 1965 I bought all the Pitcairn stamps from 1940 to date, mint and lightly hinged, for $12.50, and those of Norfolk Island (lacking only five low-value stamps) in similar condition for the same figure. A glance at the catalogue will reveal the extent of the bargain by today's prices, but at that date the material was not sought after and I had no competition for my bid. Certainly similar bargains of other countries are still being offered, and will continue to turn up in the future.

If you have unpopular material or split sets or small accumulations which dealers will not buy and which are not worth advertising, you will be able to get rid of most at a small auction (although your profit may well be small). The really good items, certain of widespread competition, are best placed in the better class of auction, where they may make considerable sums. Mint sheets are best kept out of auctions, as they are likely to be bought by other investors who are interested only in reselling at a speedy profit and so are not prepared to bid highly: such items are best sold through advertising direct to the collector and investor at just *below* normal retail prices.

What about the straightforward one-country collection?

By and large a simple stamp collection is not usually a good investment item. It may sell for a sensible price if it is in fine condition and offered at a good auction, but my own quotations for the Pitcairn and Norfolk collections are proof that such material usually realizes only a low figure. If the country is popular, of course, the collection could be offered by advertisement; careful study of the market will give the seller an idea of what his material is likely to fetch—but unless market prices have risen dramatically he has little hope of realizing more than it cost to build up the collection set by set from retail sources.

A final point about auctions: Remember that the vendor pays the auctioneer's commission, so take this into account before you fix your price for material offered for sale.

SENSIBLE

INVESTMENT

As a new collector or investor, you are wholeheartedly urged to start by just building up a fairly general collection, without any thought of making a profit from it. Use your time to become acquainted with stamp dealers, catalogues, magazines, and the many intricacies of the market. This study will give you a good idea of where your interests really lie, and how to apply the tips given in this book to your chosen specialty.

During this initial period, steer clear of large disbursements and do not involve yourself too deeply in any single country; you haven't yet the experience to avoid making mistakes, but you can at least see to it that your errors are small ones. The fruit of this period may well be an attractive collection, perhaps worth selling within a short period, but it is in effect a child's primer to philately.

When at last you come to make a real start, you will know better where to go, what to spend, and what to do with the material you buy. Start your permanent collection carefully, cannily, and with flair.

First, pick your countries. Make your choice by considering the present market conditions, picking perhaps one country which is currently very popular and two or three sidelines which are not in the limelight. For the first-choice country, material will be plentiful in the lower ranges, but the competition will be fierce for better items; with the smaller countries, expect to experience difficulty right from the start. If at the same time a topical collection is started, this should be chosen mainly as a relaxation and not with a view to immediate profit.

In deciding on the countries, give close attention to the philatelic policy of the issuing authorities, and to quantities printed and postally used. The other points we have dealt with are also of great importance, but if these two alone are unfavorable, forget it! Bear in mind recent market tips and articles in the philatelic press. If much has recently been written about your sideline countries, it may be that a rise in popularity is imminent and you will be too late on the scene to make a killing or even to build up a reasonable collection at a low cost.

Don't, at this stage, decide to collect only mint or only used stamps—take the lot. In time you may find that one or the other offers the best investment, but you will probably end up by disposing of your mint stamps *en bloc* and, if you have chosen well and bought carefully, probably at a good price.

Before you sign on with a new-issue dealer, write to the Philatelic Bureau in the country and buy *all* the issues they have in stock. Collectors are often astonished to discover that issues long withdrawn are still available there at face value. For example, the Ethiopian bureau still offers a selection of sets from 1947 onward! If you do not know where to write, address your letter to the Postmaster General, asking him to pass it on to the proper department. Also available are directories of official bureaus and sources of new-issue material, some of which include extensive lists of dealers and auctioneers.

Next, place your standing order for new issues with a reputable dealer who can supply not only straightforward issues but also postal stationery, officials and postage-dues, and any other relevant sidelines. If necessary, make arrangements direct with the country of origin to obtain difficult material. Do *not* allow yourself to be fobbed off with the excuse of a lazy or uninterested dealer that he "cannot get this material." If he can't, go elsewhere, pay more, but make sure you get it all.

Keep a very close eye on all new-issue announcements and do not hesitate to chase your supplier if you feel he may overlook a particular variety. Such an example occurred with the issue of three Pitcairn stamps in 1968, commemorating the 150th anniversary of the death of Captain Bligh. Sheets of the 1¢ value supplied by the Crown Agents came from a different printing from those sent to the island, and most dealers slipped up badly in that they supplied their clients with the mint set of the Crown Agents issue and the used set from the island stocks—naturally the scarce items are the local-release mint and the C.A. values used! Although not listed by Scott's, this variety is recognized by specialist collectors and is highly sought after. The British firm of Gibbons list both shades in their *Elizabethan* catalogue, pricing the C.A. release at 8 cents and the islands issue at 66 cents—quite a difference, and even this only hints at the real problem, which is to find both types in "imprint blocks" showing the printer's name in a totally different color, or cylinder number blocks where the order in which the colors are printed varies.

If your dealer cannot supply such scarce items, you should without hesitation order copies from any dealer advertising them or, if necessary, direct from the country. Don't worry about duplication; if your dealer can't supply, others will be in the same position, and you should have little difficulty in disposing of extra copies at a handsome profit either through the trade or to other collectors who have been let down.

In any case, whenever you feel that a particular issue— whether inside or outside your normal field (though you should be wary of areas in which your expertise is nil)—is going to be a winner, by all means play your hunch and place advance orders for extra copies (or sheets, if that is the way you collect). Immediacy is what counts—get in before the others do.

However, with any material bought purely for investment, you must make absolutely sure that you turn over your stock before the market goes cold. In the case of long-term investment, of course, this doesn't apply, but with speculated new issues there is always a short period when everybody wants them and this is the time for you to sell, at a reasonable mark-up, rather than hanging on for further rises which may never come.

In planning your expenditure, weigh the cost to buy first-day covers and maximum cards (which always carry a sizable premium over the value of the stamps) against possible future profits. Don't overweigh your collection with these, but use your own judgment and then stick to it. I am not going to make any recommendations either way about these, but if you do obtain them, and you see what appears to be a sudden peak in popularity caused by speculation or by a short-lived topical craze, don't hesitate to sell them immediately. Whatever they are, these items are *not* of purist philatelic interest, and should be treated solely as investment stock.

The American collector should certainly take up all new U.S. issues as they appear, just for the sake of completeness, but this is less a matter of investment than of keeping in touch with the times. Some very interesting things are happening in the production of U.S. stamps, which may well throw light on future developments elsewhere, and it pays to keep a close eye on any innovations.

U.S. issues do not offer scarce varieties in watermark and perforation which make speedy purchase necessary, and printing quantities are always adequate and usually massive. The purchase of first-day covers, maximum cards, and similar sidelines is a matter of personal taste, but the idea of salting away full sheets of stamps is a sheer misuse of money which could be far better employed in almost any other field of philately.

Whatever you do, don't try to cover too many countries, and don't sell out and start up again on a whim. A collection should be sold only when it has matured: anything else is selling short and should only be resorted to in case of dire necessity. Then again, forced sales, especially when carried out hurriedly, rarely provide a good return, so do be careful.

In the case of your minor countries, by all means acquire cheap flaws and varieties as they come to hand. Here you are not being forced by popular demand to pay high prices, and in the course of time these unconsidered trifles may come to demand considerable prices as popularity brings the country to the forefront of the market.

As soon as you have arranged for your new issues, *join a specialist society*. These words are so important that I would like to see them printed in gold. Don't worry that you are a novice; don't feel that you can leave it until later. And don't be put off when you find that the bulletin is over your head. Register now, and make the most you can of the society's services. If you can't find a society for your country, write to philatelic journals for information, ask your dealer, or even advertise for other collectors to get in touch with you.

Subscribe to a good magazine; read the news pages and the tipster's column, and read all the articles, even if they are outside your field—there is always something to be learned from other countries which may throw light on your own area. In the advertisement columns, study the offers and prices carefully, noting especially what is *not* being offered. Scanning the ads will keep you closely in touch with the market; here you can pick up the material you need, and learn how and when to sell your investment material.

Now you are starting to work backward to older issues. Don't just do this chronologically: make certain you have every tipped item first of all—they are unlikely to become cheaper! Then acquire every item which, from details of quantities printed and used, appears to be underpriced in the catalogue. Don't give up the chase if you can't find them: this is the reason for the low market activity. Make sure you pick up any other material you are offered which is cheap, even if you don't really want it at the time—you will one day, and then you'll be glad you took the chance.

Never assume that you are not going to touch first-flight covers, or sea post, or pre-adhesive items, or whatever it may be. You will sooner or later, if they add interest and value to your collection. This is another good reason for restricting the number of countries right from the start: you will avoid the problem of "Which can I afford?" and you will become more expert more quickly. At the same time, keep your investment lines going: you are going to need these sooner or later, when faced with the purchase of a cover or stamp which costs ten times what you can afford. Don't pass it by—sell out and get it now.

Have your name and specialty recorded with as many specialized dealers as you can locate. Attendance at annual exhibitions will give you the chance to meet a great number of dealers under one roof and to discover what they have in stock that never appears in their advertisements. Never be afraid to ask for what you want, and be as precise as you can: even if the dealer says he cannot supply your needs, insist that he take note of them—he may be offered the material the next day. Remember that a dealer is unlikely to buy offbeat material unless he has an outlet for it: if your name is on his lists, and your wants are clearly set out, he is more likely to purchase items you want.

Keep an eye open for new issues which seem as though they might be the start of new topics: put aside a few sets of these, and you may find that you are one of the few to do so, especially if they are from unpopular countries. On the other hand, be very wary of deliberately engineered issues from agency countries, for which there is unlikely to be a great demand. And, most of all, steer clear of speculated items unless you are there before the speculators!

Read all you can about your chosen country and its posts; build up your postal-history collection as speedily and cheaply as you can, and do not hesitate with less popular countries to make contacts with local dealers and collectors in the country who may turn up odd items for you. In the meantime, try to fill the gaps in your collection—preferably in full sets, as there is no point in buying odd values if you later have to buy the whole set to get the rest.

Pay particular attention to any regular issue which has been on sale for only a very short time before withdrawal or replacement; the same applies to provisionals and some-times to the basic stamps which have been overprinted. These are the items to watch, the dark horses of the set: if you feel so inclined, you could put away blocks of four, or even more, of such varieties in anticipation of a market rise. After all, you are the expert here—you should know which are going to be the tips of tomorrow.

Maintain your contacts, exhibit your collection, and just keep going. You will have a marvelous time, you will become an expert, you will in time gain recognition, and you will be building up a really worthwhile collection—philatelically and for investment.

If you can write, do so. Short notes on new discoveries for your specialist society or for the general philatelic press are always welcome, but they must be *news*. Short general articles on your country, provided they concentrate on the philately and not the countryside, are always needed. If you can prepare a learned paper, submit it to a learned journal. And if you are the first man to catalogue the varieties or the postal history of a country, then you have it made.

Stamp collecting is a marvelous hobby, and anyone can enjoy it. It can be a profitable one, but that takes care, study, and canniness: cultivate these qualities and your collection, as well as your pocket, will gain from it.

WHAT DOES

IT COST?

A STAMP COLLECTION costs just as much as you want it to cost. Your expenditure is fitted to your pocket, and can range from as little as $2 a week to many thousands of dollars a year.

For a rough guide on new issues alone, take a catalogue and add up the *face* value of all the stamps issued for your countries during the past three years: this will probably be an increasing figure, as more stamps appear every year. Add the dealer's commission, double it for one mint stamp plus one used, add the probable cost of first-day covers and maximum cards if you are going to take these as well, and you have a rough idea of your future costs for new issues alone.

Then total up the *catalogue* value of every stamp ever issued, noting separately each stamp catalogued at, say, $10 or more. You can expect to pay—by careful buying—perhaps 50 percent of catalogue price for all these, maybe less; for the few really good stamps you may have to pay more, but you will save on all the unconsidered low values which are priced highly in the catalogue merely because of handling charges, and which you will be able to pick up in a one-country packet for very little. This gives you an idea of your total expenditure, at today's prices, and will show you at a glance which stamps you must get now or never and which can wait.

Next you must find out the extent of the postal history— how many post offices, how far back you must go, how scarce is the material, where you can get it. Allow perhaps $1 per cover for the run-of-the-mill items (many will be cheaper) and as much as $20 to $50 for really difficult items. Items priced much higher than this you may have to ignore entirely for some time.

Now that you have an approximate idea of your probable total expenditure over a period of years, don't be put off by the sum—if your investment material is carefully selected it will help you over most of the rough spots. At least it will show you whether your task is feasible or is going to be totally impossible, and you can take further action from there.

On the investment side, again you will spend what you can afford. If you are prepared to disburse thousands of dollars annually, then the best advice is to buy single, certificated, classic items, particularly postal-history material, which are assured of steady improvement merely because there are too few men of wealth and discernment to upset this rarefied market but a sufficient number of wealthy advanced students to keep prices moving up by their continued demand.

If your investment is only, say, $2 a week at first, don't despair: put it into sets of new issues, or anything which you feel will produce a good—I might say an *assured*— mark-up fairly quickly, and then turn these over for ever bigger and better items. Whatever you do, don't follow the market: lead it, and *don't* put all your eggs in one basket.

And always keep the two sides of your philatelic spending—for your collection and for investment—strictly apart, even though you can look on your collection itself as being a long-term investment.

EFFECTS OF

INVESTMENT

As PHILATELIC INVESTMENT depends on market movements, so the market is affected by investment in stamps. Of all the stamps issued in the world, a large proportion disappear very speedily from the market. They are used on letters and destroyed, or are hoarded by people who will never part with them and will probably treat them so badly that they will become worthless. They are absorbed into junior collections and ruined, or they are spoiled by bad storage or handling. A small quantity find their way into specialist collections where they will stay for many years, and many more are taken up by straightforward collectors and only briefly reappear on the market.

It is only the balance which is taken up by investors. Some of the material will remain in dealers' stocks, but as we have seen, ideally the dealer will try to turn over his stocks speedily. Because dealers' stocks are open to investment offers at all times, they in effect form part of the bulk of investment stocks. The important thing for the investor to know is the way in which this material is held—by how many people, in how many countries, in what bulk per investor, with what speed it can be expected to reappear on the market, and in what quantities.

Always strive to see your own investment material from the viewpoint of the world's total holdings. If material is thinly spread over a large number of people, there is little chance that a great deal will come on the market at any one time, and the investment potential is therefore safeguarded against panic selling. If individual investors hold large stocks, there is the chance that too much may come on the market at one time to be immediately absorbed; this may cause a slight drop in prices, which in turn may bring even more material onto the market at panic prices, precipitating a slump.

For this reason, popular material should be bought for short-term appreciation only; with the swing of popularity, the price is eventually going to stabilize at a lower level anyway. Unpopular material can be kept for many years in the hope of a rise, especially when one is relatively sure that no really large stocks exist anywhere whose appearance is likely to affect prices.

It is where very large quantities of a particular issue are held by a single person or firm that one should exercise extreme caution, and this is where some agency-controlled countries are suspect. At the time of issue, and sometimes before, it is not unknown for a subsidiary company of the agency to buy the greater part of an issue, at advantageous prices, with the aim of releasing the stamps on the market in small regular quantities over a period of years. Should the existence of such speculator stocks not be generally known, there is always the chance that the company will tire of waiting and will swamp the market with the material, selling short for reinvestment.

The day of the one-man speculation is now, happily, almost past, but the story of one such planned operation will show the dangers. A small trader in the Cook Islands in 1935 was intrigued by the forthcoming Silver Jubilee issue, which in the islands was to comprise 1d., 2½d., and 6d. overprinted stamps. The issue was limited, quantities being 136,400 of the 1d. stamp, 98,080 of the 2½d., and 107,520 of the 6d. As can be seen, the smallest quantity was of the 2½d. value, and the total face value of these was (at the then current rate of exchange) $4,904.

The bulk of the stamps was to be placed on sale in the islands, with small quantities offered at the philatelic counters in four New Zealand towns. It was the trader's plan to have friends at the head of the line in Wellington, Auckland, Christchurch, and Dunedin, while other friends in the islands would be ready to purchase stamps there as they arrived. His aim was to acquire every copy of the 2½d. value for less than $5,000!

Had the scheme been carried out, there is no doubt that in a remarkably short time the speculator would have been able to demand upward of $3.50 each for the stamps. After all, this was the Silver Jubilee issue, sought at ever-increasing prices during succeeding months by dealers and collectors throughout the world. And at $3.50 each the trader's profit would have been seventy-fold—that is, he would have shown 7000 percent improvement on his investment.

But this was in the days of the Depression, and the trader was unable to raise the cash, partly because his colleagues just could not bring themselves to believe that such a profit was possible. In the end, he had just $245 to spend, which he used to buy full sets of the issue. Some of these he affixed to covers, some he kept mint. Six months later he accepted $2,340 for the lot. Even this works out to an 850 percent profit over his investment, which shows that the original plan was by no means visionary!

The danger in a situation like this is that the speculator may buy up 90 percent of the stocks; the remaining 10 percent will rise to dizzy heights, but if he unloads all at once, and if the supply is then too large for the market to absorb, prices will plummet. The appearance of such relatively large quantities even on a market far from saturation can have a most unsettling effect and can destroy the real investment value of the remainder.

Such speculation tends to bring the trade into disrepute

with many investors and collectors who are not sufficiently *au fait* with the market to realize just what has happened. The bad publicity can be extremely harmful to philately both as investment and as a hobby, and the trade is united in its attempts to stop speculation, or if it occurs to denounce it and—so far as the laws of libel allow—to warn collectors off such issues.

On the other side of the coin are the constant attempts of the trade, the societies, and collectors in general to publicize philately and to attract new collectors. The more new collectors there are, the less material will be available to investors—and so the value of the remaining stock is improved. And inasmuch as many new collectors eventually become specialists and investors, they join the battle and so help prices rise still further. It is thus in the interests of every collector to become an enthusiastic ambassador for the hobby.

In the United States, where the market is heavily slanted toward the issues of a few countries, diversification is to be encouraged, and the health of the hobby can be improved by strenuous efforts to wean newer collectors away from modern domestic issues and into the equally attractive and more profitable field of postal history and the collection of foreign stamps from reputable countries. Here is a mission fit for every collector to espouse, for his own good and for the good of philately itself.

THE INTERNATIONAL

MARKET

OBVIOUSLY, popularity differs from country to country, and stamps which are almost unwanted in the United States may fetch high prices elsewhere. This is one of the reasons for the difference in catalogue values found in overseas publications. Because stamps of certain countries are just not available in the United States, the collector must order from abroad, joining in the battle with local enthusiasts for material and buying at prices far higher than he would expect to pay at home. Certainly this must be considered when he makes his original choice of countries, although it may on occasion be worth his while to pay the higher prices and wait for the effect of a delayed popularity at home to push up the international market even higher. By adhering to this rule many collectors and dealers have made substantial profits.

On the other hand, if the popularity dies without infecting the home market, he may be left with material bought at high prices which it will take many years to reach again as the pendulum swings back. This does not happen frequently in the United States, where new fads almost immediately attract a devoted following; this is, however, another result of the narrow approach of American collectors. There are many examples of such inflated material suddenly losing its international support, leaving the unin-

formed U.S. collector high and dry with only his own com-
patriots to take up the slack.

The international nature of the stamp market means that
it is also susceptible to fluctuations in world currency. For
the Israeli collector, for example, this has meant constantly
rising costs in keeping up his hobby, while the many deval-
uations of his currency have from time to time thrown upon
the market vast amounts of Israeli stamps and postal material at prices significantly below the previous levels. It is
only thanks to the country's remarkable resiliency, and the
amount of U.S. investment there, that the market has rallied
on each occasion and climbed back to even higher levels.

When the pound was devalued in 1967, British dealers
found that overnight their cost to buy from abroad had
risen by one-sixth. This rapidly brought higher retail prices
all around, to the benefit of the investor in overseas material,
whose holdings had appreciated by one-sixth without any
action on his part. In fact, many dealers tried to peg the rise,
and continued to sell their existing stocks at pre-devaluation
prices. But restocking automatically brought rises, and soon
the market stabilized at the higher level—with the exception of those issues from countries which had devalued at
the same time as Britain, where other, more complex factors
had an effect.

This example is but one of many in which fiscal changes
in one country have affected the international stamp market,
and the U.S. collector should certainly be aware of currency
changes throughout the world in order to take advantage
of all movements which favor expenditure at short notice
or which, on the other hand, may be a warning to sell short
and cut possible losses.

There is another side to this picture, so far as the devaluation of the pound was concerned: from that date,
stamps held in Britain could in theory be purchased by
collectors in other countries for one-seventh less money in
their own currency than before, since in real terms that was

the drop in the value of the pound. The British market was buoyant enough to weather the storm, and prices for British material continued upward. However, for other items it was for a time well worth the while of any overseas collector to purchase at current British prices whatever he could find, and it speaks well for the stability of the British market that this did not lead to a rush of material from the country. One of the major advantages to the philatelic world was that devaluation helped cushion the British market against the worst effects of the recession in German and Swiss stamps which occurred at that time.

The strength of the philatelic market lies in the international appeal of stamps and postal history, and the fluctuations in popularity and demand make it an ever-moving and ever-interesting field of study. The newcomer to philately can look forward to untold hours of pleasure in the hobby and, it is the author's hope, a handsome return on his capital.

Good hunting!

SUBJECT INDEX

187

COUNTRY INDEX

Aden (Aden States), 112
Afghanistan, 60, 130
Africa, 116, 124, 129. *See also* specific countries by name
Albania, 42
Algeria, 129, 130, 145
Andorra, 126
Anguilla, 112
Antarctic, 114-15, 118
Antigua, 112
Argentina, 120
Ascension Islands, 112
Asia, 130-31. *See also* specific countries by name
Australia, 21-22, 49, 53, 58, 90, 112-15, 119, 138
Austria, 93, 127
Azores, 127

Barbuda, 115
Basutoland (now Lesotho), 116
Bechuanaland (now Botswana), 116
Belgium, 27, 88, 126-27
Bolivia, 120-21
Brazil, 121

British Commonwealth, 41, 107, 108, 112-19. *See also* specific countries by name
British Guiana (now Guyana), 55, 117
British Indian Ocean Territory, 117
Brunei, 116
Burma, 117

Cambodia, 130, 131
Canada, 117-18
Canal Zone, 107
Caroline Islands, 125
Central African Republic, 124
Ceylon, 117
Chile, 120-21, 145
China, 46, 97, 130
Colombia, 120-21
Communist bloc nations, 21, 46, 53-54, 91, 97, 123, 128-29. *See also* specific countries by name
Confederate states (U.S.), 110, 136
Cook Islands, 28, 36, 61, 67, 118, 180-81
Cuba, 46, 108, 121

190